THE DIVINE PITY

Famous books and authors in the Fontana Series

The
Divine Pity

A Study in
The Social Implications
of the Beatitudes

GERALD VANN, O.P.

COLLINS

fontana books

First published 1945
First issued in Fontana Books 1956

PRINTED IN GREAT BRITAIN
COLLINS CLEAR-TYPE PRESS: LONDON AND GLASGOW

CONTENTS

CHAPTER I

THE SEARCH FOR LIFE

ONE of the most tantalizing figures in the whole of the Gospel story is surely Lazarus, the man who for four days lay dead, and was then brought back to the world by the word of our Lord. He was a man who knew by experience, who had *seen,* the answer to the questions which perpetually engage the human mind : the nature of the world that awaits us beyond the tomb. And yet perhaps even if he had spoken and his words had come down to us we should not be much the wiser; for we have the testimony of St. Paul that it is idle to hope for an expression of the inexpressible : " eye hath noth seen, nor ear heard, neither hath it entered into the heart of a man. . . ."

But there is another question which vexes the mind; and to this we might well have expected an answer. What difference did his journey into eternity make to him, how did it alter his way of life when he returned to the world of time? Here, too, we are left baffled and without an answer; we are told nothing further of him at all, except that when, later on, Jesus went to Bethany and a supper was made for Him, Lazarus was one of the guests. But what was he like? How was he changed? And perhaps, in default of information, we paint a picture of him for ourselves : we tend to think that with this unforgettable taste of infinity forever with him he must necessarily have been dreamy, preoccupied, hopelessly bored with the unimportance, the pettiness, of the business of living, the everyday affairs of the world of men. You imagine the practical, motherly Martha having to tell him repeatedly at meal-times : " Lazarus, do get on with your food."

And yet there was a supper, and he was one of the guests.

Was he, in fact, dreamy, abstracted, bored? Fortunately
we need not be at a loss for an authentic answer; for if
Lazarus himself does not supply one there are plenty who
do.   There are plenty of others who, like him in what
matters most, have known eternity and then returned to
the world of time: there are all the saints who have been
given in the heights of prayer to know the secret things of
God and in their ecstasy have forgotten everything but the
Eternal, but who then returned again to the world of man
—and were they dreamy, were they bored and preoccupied?
There was St. Paul who was rapt to the seventh heaven;
and thereafter swept like a blazing fire through the length
and breadth of the world. There was St. Teresa, living
with God in the heights of the prayer of union, yet always
returning again to the busy, practical life of organization.
The list could be prolonged indefinitely. What is the explanation? Why is it that the picture we tend to paint for
ourselves is so entirely at variance with the facts? For
indeed we could surely appeal in support of it to common
human experience: the man who has been through some
intense experience does, in fact, tend to be preoccupied.
We shall find the answer in the most striking and explicit
parallel to the experience of Lazarus: the story of St.
Catherine of Siena.

We are told that one day when her confessor was preaching a sermon in the church they brought news to him that
Catherine was dead. He went round to her house, where
her followers were gathered weeping; but he, for his part,
refused, in spite of the appearances, to believe that she was
dead, and after a time she did indeed return to the world
and open her eyes and become aware of what was going on
around her.   Now her first words were much what we
should have expected: for a long time she could only cry,
over and over again, " Oh, I am so unhappy," because she
had seen the secret things of God and could not bear to be
parted again from them. But that is not the whole story:
far from it.

For it was Catherine who, after this "mystical death,"
became one of the most famous and the most powerful
women of her century, endlessly active, advising Popes and
princes, travelling, negotiating, issuing orders, determining
policies, shaping the life of Christendom. What had inter-
vened? She had learned the truth expressed in the words
of the pseudo-Denys: *omnium divinorum divinissimum est
cooperare Deo in salutem animarum:* of all divine things
the most divine is to share with God in the saving of souls;
she had begged our Lord in ecstasy to take her back to her
eternal home, and she had been reproached by Him—for
her *egoism.* She had been taught by Him: "You cannot
render Me any service but you can help your neighbour.
The soul in love with My truth gives herself no rest but
searches ceaselessly to help others. You cannot give back
to me Myself the love I demand, but I have put you beside
your neighbour so that you may do for him what you cannot do for Me. What you do for your neighbour, then I
consider as being done for Me."

And finally, there is the astonishing story of the exchange
of hearts: the story that one day our Lord took her heart
from her, and some days later gave her, instead, His own,
so that from that time forward she always prayed: My
Lord, I offer Thee *Thy* heart; and the substantial reality
that we must see in this story, and apply to ourselves, is the
fact that to have the heart of Christ means to be identified
with the will of Christ: to will nothing that Christ does
not will, to will everything that He does will. And what
is the supreme desire of the will of the Christ who is Lover
and Saviour, but to obey and glorify God by redeeming the
world?

Why, then, do we go wrong in our judgement about the
saint returning from eternity in the world of time? Because
we forget, or under-estimate, the importance of the world.
We forget, first of all, its importance as praising God. They
tell us of another Dominican saint, Bl. Jordan of Saxony,
that one day as he was walking with some of his students

along a country road, an ermine darted across into the
hedge a few yards in front of them, and the youths, who
had never seen one before, were disappointed at the short
glimpse they had caught of it. Jordan went to the side of
the road and called to the little animal to come out and let
them have a look at it. It obeyed; put its front paws on
his hand; let itself be stroked. Then Jordan blessed it, and
bade it go back and praise God. The saints' lives are full
of similar stories, because they remember the thing we forget : that the world is God's handiwork and His habitation,
and that its destiny is to praise Him. " Bless the Lord, all
ye works of the Lord " : the lilies of the field praise Him
with their whiteness and the grass with its green; the birds
of the air bless Him with the beauty of their flight, the
beasts of the field bless Him in their work and their play.
But these are not isolated voices raised to God; they are
part of the total song of the spheres, the song of all creation;
for it is creation in its order and unity and wholeness which
best reflects the beauty of God. And man has, in this sym-
phony of nature, a special, a directive, part to play; it is for
him, first of all, to join in the song with immortal voice
himself; but it is for him also to help with his husbandry
the song of the lesser creation, and to raise it by his awareness and his loving worship of God to a more explicit
sharing in the prayer of Christ—*instaurare omnia in
Christo.*

It is no mean thing, this song of the spheres, and the part
which each creature plays in it : it was for this that the
world was made. And when you return from prayer to the
homely things of earthly life it is this you must see in them :
if you are tempted to be bored with them, remind yourself
of this. You are called with all the saints, to bless in the
power of Christ's priesthood the song of the world, and to
perfect it. But there is much more than this. There is sin
in the world. The song of creation is out of harmony : there
are voices which are faulty or mute or discordant : the world
of nature, as St. Paul reminds us, is still in travail, and the

world of man is still sunk in sin and ignorance and malice:
there is work to be done in the world by those who love
God, redemptive work, and for that work God *needs* them.
The more you understand what this song of creation means,
the more you will realise how imperfect sin has made it.
But the more deeply you have become identified with the
heart of Christ, the more you will want to help in redeeming creation and restoring the perfection of the song. And
you can only redeem and restore in the degree to which,
being first redeemed and restored yourself, you have learned
to love.

Here is the clue to that paradox which runs right through
the teachings of our Lord, the lives of the saints, the sayings
of the mystics. " Honour thy father and thy mother," " by
this shall all men know that you are my disciples, if you
have love one for another "; " if any man come to me and
hate not his father and mother and wife and children and
brethren and sisters . . . he cannot be my disciple." How
can we love and yet hate? How can we, with St. Paul,
suffer " the loss of all things and count them but as dung,"
and yet, also with St. Paul, be " all things to all men "?
St. Paul himself tells us when he says " I live, now not I,
but Christ liveth in me." St. Thomas tells us when, quoting
the words of our Lord, he writes: " We must hate those
near to us for God's sake, i.e. if they turn us away from
God." There is no answer other than an exchange of hearts
with Christ; but in the exchange of hearts with Christ there
is an answer which is total, all-embracing, final.

You must give all to God, you must surrender everything,
you must strip yourself of every vestige of self-will—it is
the common teaching of all the saints and mystics. You
must have no will in regard to created things but the will
of God. You must enter into nothingness, and naked follow
the naked Christ. But that does not mean that you may
refuse creatures their rights, as things in themselves, as
God's handiwork, as part of the song of the spheres : it does
not mean that you may shuffle off your responsibilities, that

you may refuse to love what God loves. M. Maritain, in some magnificent and invaluable pages of *Les Degrés du Savoir,* has shown, first of all the danger—a danger of total misunderstanding—which lies in confusing the language of mysticism with the language of theology; and secondly, the way in which theology can, in fact, state with perfect clarity the single truth in which the apparently opposing commands of love and hatred are made one. When St. John of the Cross, he writes, bids his readers tear up by the very root all attachment to their families, " are we to suppose that he is contradicting the common teaching of the Church, and notably of St. Thomás, on the love that is due to them? On the contrary, he is presupposing this teaching. He knows that his readers are no more likely to fall into insensibility than the contemplatives to whom he teaches the way of nothingness are likely to fall into quietism. . . . These prescriptions must be taken in all their force, without the least softening-down. But we have to understand them. They demand not only an external detachment but an internal, radical, detachment, a complete death : but this means a radical renunciation of our *proprietorship* and *purely natural exercise* of our feelings, a renunciation thanks to which a greater love will vivify them. It does *not* mean a radical destruction of the (ontological) *reality,* if one may speak thus, of those feelings in themselves. Between these two sorts of death there is all the distance between the superhuman and the inhuman : as far as the growth in the life of the spirit is concerned, it is as great a disaster to abandon oneself to the second, and become hardshelled and cold of heart . . . as it is to reject the first, which means to refuse the perfection of love and the value to be set on it."*

The " expropriation of the self," dying, in the words of St. Bernard, " the death of the angels " : this is the meaning of all that the saints have to say of Christian detachment.

*Cf. J. Maritain: *Les Degrés du Savoir.* Annexe IX : *Les* Cautelas *de saint Jean de la Croix,* pp. 903-4. (This appendix is not printed, unfortunately, in the English edition.)

St. John "preaches neither mutilation nor suicide, nor the slightest ontological destruction of the most fragmentary filament of the wing of the smallest gnat. He is not concerned with the structure of our substance and its faculties; his is concerned with our *proprietorship of ourselves,* as expressed in the use we make of our active power as free and morally responsible beings. And there he demands everything of us. There we have to give everything. What he does preach is a very real death, a death much more subtle and delicate than any material death or destruction : the death which is called the *expropriation of the self.* This destruction of self-will is a death which is active and effective within our being, a death which is experienced and freely undergone; it is within the innermost activity of the spirit that it takes place, and by the spirit that it is brought about. It grows with the growth of the spirit, and cleaves to it in its inmost depths. But it is a death which does not destroy sensitivity, but, on the contrary, refines it, and makes it more exquisite. It does not harden the fibres of the being, but, on the contrary, makes them supple, and spiritualizes them. It is a death which transforms us into love."*

And what follows? The more the saint burns out of his heart everything that savours of a proprietary attitude to creatures, every vestige, therefore, of self-love, in other words the more he "despises creatures in the degree to which they are rivals to God or objects of a possible choice against God, the more he cherishes them in and for Him whom he loves, inasmuch as they are loved by Him. . . . For to love a being in and for God—I am speaking here of the love of friendship, not of the love of covetousness—is not to treat it as a pure means or occasion for loving God. That would mean excusing oneself from loving it in itself —and if we do that we cease immediately to love God truly,

---

*Maritain, *op cit.* p. 659; English transl. p. 407. (In this and the following quotations I have made use of the English edition, but have departed from it a good deal in places.)

for we only truly love Him if we love also His visible
images. No, to love a being in and for God is to love it in
itself, and to treat it as an end, and to desire its good precisely because in itself and for itself it is worthy of love. ....
This is the explanation of the paradox whereby in the end
the saint enfolds in a universal love of friendship and piety
—incomparably more care-free but also more tender and
more happy than the possessive love of the voluptuary or
the miser—everything which passes with time, all the weakness and the beauty of things, all that he has abandoned."*

But again what follows? We tend to think of wisdom as
something wholly still, withdrawn, absorbed; but we are
told in the Bible, on the contrary, that it is " more active
than all active things." We are here at the very key-note, on
the practical side, of christian contemplation. For it is
through Christ that the christian mystic comes to God; it is
through Christ the Lover and Redeemer of men; and
having, through Christ, ascended to the Father, he cannot
forget the suffering world which until the end of time is the
preoccupation of the heart of Christ: " the grace itself
which transforms us is the grace of our crucified Lord, and
it is in order that we may share in the work that is His own,
that is, to die for the world, that we are transfigured from
brightness into brightness."† So we find Catherine, her
momentary egoism long outlived, longing to bear all the
sorrows of the whole world on her shoulders, we find her,
in fact, burdened with all the weight of the ship of the
Church, we find her offering to Christ the heart of Christ,
and therewith the love that was satisfied only when it broke
upon the Cross.

So there are the two things, which are but two comple-
mentary aspects of a single life: there is the complete and
utter dispossession of the self of all that is not God, so that
in truth you can say " I live, now not I, but Christ liveth
in me "—the heart of Christ, the will of Christ, the power

* Maritain, op cit. pp. 665-6; English transl. p. 411.
† op. cit. p. 662; English transl. p. 409.

of Christ. And there is at the same time what is precisely
implied in those words : the fullness of love, the super-
abundance of life, the desire to work and suffer, even unto
death, for the world that is loved with the love of Christ,
a love which leaves nothing outside, a love for which
nothing is too small, too poor, too weak, too full of sin.

Let us return to Catherine. The exchange of hearts is for
her a beginning—it is what makes possible the immensity
of her love and labours and power in the world. But it is
also an end, a consummation. It is a consummation in the
sense that it is the conclusion of a long, and terrifyingly
arduous process of expropriation of the self : to that aspect
of it we must turn in a moment. But it is a consummation
also, and primarily, because it is in fact the very stuff of
human destiny. " Seek ye first the kingdom of God " : we
must not think of contemplation as a means to action, even
the highest action; contemplation is not a means to an end,
but is itself the end—an end so rich and full of superabun-
dant life that, in fact, it is inevitably expressed in action as
the vision of the artist or the lover is expressed in stone or
paint, in word and gesture. We shall never be saints if we
ignore our responsibilities to the world, forget the law of
love, close the bowels of our mercy against our brother, and
try to build for ourselves a private and selfish beatitude.
" By this shall men know that you are my disciples, if you
have love one for another "; " if any man say : I love God,
and hateth his brother; he is a liar. For he that loveth not
his brother whom he seeth, how can he love God whom he
seeth not?" And Ruysbroeck : " Be kind, be kind, and you
will be saints." Be kind : it is easy to be kind to our friends;
but where shall we find the ability to be kind to *all*, to be
kind to the people who irritate us, the people who attack
and despise and malign us? We shall find it only in the
heart of Christ.

And that is why, if it is a total misunderstanding of the
Gospel to suppose that we are to seek our own sanctification, our own perfection, and ignore the needs of the world,

ignore the very purpose of the human life of Christ, it is also a total misunderstanding to suppose that we can work for the world, as christians, and so become saints, without being identified with Christ. "Unless the grain of wheat falling into the ground die, itself remaineth alone." We must not wait until we are wholly transformed into Christ before attempting to share in His work in the world—if we did we should have little to offer Him, most of us, when we died. It is a logical, not a temporal, order. But unless we try more and more, every day, to make our work in the world an expression of our love of God; unless we try to make every thought and desire and action more and more completely identical with the mind and will of God, our work may remain our work instead of His, and then it will be of little value, and we may even commit the blasphemy of confusing end with means, and subordinating the love of God to the love of men.

The exchange of hearts is the consummation of a long and agonizing process: it is no easy thing to die and be re-born. There are many different kinds of saints; and some we think of as fierce and some as gentle; some can find God only by withdrawing from the world to caves and desert places, and others find Him in the midst of men and in the voice of nature. But in one thing they are all equally fierce and equally unrelenting: in their struggle to expropriate the self, to kill the false self that wants to be its own master and refuses to be the child of God. For this is a thing in which there can be no half-measures. It is the whole heart that has to be exchanged. Sometimes there is an obvious and clear-cut choice to be made: I know that this is what I want, and that God's will is different; and you choose the will of God. That is something, but it is only a beginning. There are other choices to be made, when the thing you want is not wrong in itself and yet may not be God's will for you at this particular moment: and if you can school yourself to choose always the will of God in these things, that is something much more. But still it is only a begin-

ning. You have not yet allowed the power of God to transform you wholly into Christ. You must learn to be able to
say *beforehand,* of whatever may befall, that your will is to
do the will of Him who sent you into the world to praise
Him. And you must learn to say it utterly and of everything. It means that there must be nothing, however small,
or however good, to which you would cling for a moment
against God's will: there is nothing about which you have
not already said, Thy will be done.

That is the daily struggle and death of the christian.
There is no easy way. In these days there is a growing
interest in the way of the mystic, and let us thank God for
it. But there is a danger of being misled into supposing
that to do as the mystics have done it is sufficient to evolve
a psychological technique—to learn the art of prayer without tears. There is no such thing. It is not only the mind
that has to be trained to see God. Blessed are the clean of
heart . . . The power, let us make no mistake about it,
comes only from God; and the power is offered; but to be
able to accept it we must have learned from God how to
purify the will, we must have learned the lesson of detachment. We shall pray well only in so far as we become poor
in spirit, meek, eager to suffer with Christ and for the sake
of Christ, only in so far as we can say in everything and
about everything, Thy will be done.

"Seek ye first the kingdom of God." That is the first
lesson. If we learn that lesson the rest will be added to us,
will inevitably follow. But if we think we love God's
creatures, but love them in defiance of God, we are not
loving them, we are loving ourselves. Even though we give
our bodies to be burnt for them we are not loving them, we
are loving ourselves: because we are asserting that we know
better than God what is for their good. The heart of man is
not a house that can be emptied of one set of furnishings that
another may be installed: it is not the *objects* of our love
that have to be changed, it is our *love* that has to be changed
by being transformed into the love which is the heart of

Christ. So we return to the practical hallmark of the
christian mystic : " By this shall men know that you are
my disciples . . ." The mysticism which seeks to advance
by a purely human technique, relying on human powers, is
in danger precisely of the disease of self-culture, of being
turned in upon itself, of seeking ultimately only its own
glory. But the grace which transforms the christian " is the
grace of our crucified Lord, and it is in order that we may
share in the work that is His own . . . that we are transfigured from brightness into brightness."

The world has grown old and sterile because charity has
grown cold. The love of men must grow weak and ineffective unless it is rooted in and expressive of the love of God;
the love of God also must be thought to be dwindling and
decaying into love of self unless it leads us to share in the
redeeming activity of Christ. And perhaps it is true to say
that outside the Church that zeal for doing good in the
world which is the glory of the west is losing its power because it is losing its roots in the love of God; whereas within
the Church, on the contrary, the chief danger we have to
fight against is the danger of a self-centred piety which neg-
lects its duties to the world. In the following pages, at any
rate, it is the social implications of the beatitudes which
have been mainly studied. But it is against the background
of the love of God, above all and in all, that they must be
seen. For the christian saint the love of the world does not
make sense apart from the love of God, precisely because
it is wholly and entirely an expression of the love of God.
The will to work for the world does not make sense apart
from the will of God, precisely because it is wholly and
entirely a function of obedience to the will of God. If it is
the reality of the world that we are discovering it can only
be because we are discovering the reality of God : if our
hearts are growing to fullness of love for the world it can
only be because the false self is dying and we are being
re-born in God.

It is, then, that process of being re-born—the endless day-to-day struggle to find God, to come nearer to God, to think and to will more and more exclusively as He thinks and wills—that is the *condition* of our sharing in Christ's redemptive work in the world. We shall totally misunderstand the christian way of life if we suppose that that struggle can be put on one side while we attend only to the easier task of helping humanity. It might be true to say, Take care of contemplation—make sure that it is fervent, assiduous, and wholly *God-centred*—and action will take care of itself, the redemptive work will inevitably follow in one form or another; but the reverse would certainly not be true. What is the purpose of the grace of God, the sacramental system, the whole dynamism of the supernatural life, but to enable us to know God, to love God, to serve God? That is the " one thing necessary "; that is the only complete fulfilment of the heart's desire; and the fact that if we achieve it we shall find much else included in it, must not for a moment lead us into a confusion between the relative importance of finite and Infinite.

In all that follows, then, these primary truths must be all the time presupposed and kept in mind. To be poor in spirit, to be meek, to be clean of heart; all these things denote an attitude of soul towards the world; but primarily they denote an attitude of soul towards God. The beatitudes mean, first of all, that the man who is poor in spirit and meek and clean of heart is succeeding in the essential christian struggle and so is blessed : is succeeding in the struggle to kill the false self by the daily asceticism of accepting and welcoming God's will, the struggle to find God by that daily searching and listening which is the life of prayer, and the struggle with the mind's waywardness to gain, after immense difficulty and constant failure, that abiding sense of the presence of God which is the condition of our ability to see and will all things in union with Him. Yes, we must long, and pray, and work, to be filled with the love of our

neighbour; but first of all, above all, we must long and
pray and work to possess the one thing necessary, the substance of life everlasting, the thing whereof this other, when
it is strongest and deepest, is the expression and derivative:
we must seek till we are given to find and possess, as
Catherine did, the heart of Christ.

CHAPTER II

THE BEATITUDES

GOD made us to know Him and love Him and serve Him and so to be happy.

We should not be shy of the word "happy." We have been given the gospel of life; we have been given the knowledge and love of Him who came that we might have life and have it more abundantly; we have been given the freedom of the sons of God, and though while we are on earth it is not freedom from all misery it is freedom from the deepest misery, and a prelude to the deepest happiness. St. Thomas says, in a quiet, matter-of-fact way, that "happiness is the end of life"; there is no need to argue about that, only about how we are to find happiness. And that is what the beatitudes tell us. To be suspicious of happiness and regard it as faintly irreligious is an unchristian thing—if you want to be a canonized saint you must first become a notoriously happy person—but there are ways of searching for happiness which are unchristian too. The beatitudes tell us how to be happy; and they tell us, all of them, that the way to be happy is to search for something else.

If you want to be happy, be poor in spirit, be meek, be clean of heart. They are not a question, these beatitudes, of virtue merely; St. Thomas gives us the clue to them all when he tells us that they are "certain excellent works of virtue under the impulse of the gifts of the holy Spirit, whereby we approach the goal of eternal happiness, and have a foretaste of it even in this life." Happiness is not something to be searched for; still less is it something you can make; it is something you can only receive, and become.

There are two things to notice in this definition of the beatitudes. In the first place, we are concerned with virtue in the christian sense: virtue as determined by religion and built on humility and coloured through and through by love. Because of all the labour involved in acquiring the habits of prudence, justice, and the rest, there is the same element of mastery, of the free, self-determining, independent personality, that you find in the picture of the virtues painted, let us say, by Aristotle; but that is only one aspect of christian virtue. There is man the master; but there is also always the child. To say that the virtuous action is an act of religion is to say that your attitude must be primarily one of worship, your eyes fixed on God and not on yourself. To say that love is the soul of all the virtues is to say that they are primarily a question not of doing but of being, of living in love, and that if they are not love-gifts they are not really virtue at all. And then every virtue is a form of humility: prudence, the humility of the mind that can learn and that knows that wisdom must be wooed; justice, the humility of the man who knows that every possession is also a responsibility, to God and to the world, and that he is not the absolute possessor of anything, only its steward; temperateness, the humility of the flesh, the ability to reverence and not to maul; fortitude, the humble courage which says "I can do all things" only "in Him who strengthened me."

To be humble and docile, to know the need of help and ask for it, and then to make both the asking and the acting an offering of worship and of love: this is the essential element in christian virtue, because it is this that preserves in the strength of the grown man the heart of the child.

But the beatitudes tell us that, even so, virtue is not enough. The virtuous life is imperfect so long as we fail to be fully possessed of the virtues; and the remedy for that is plainly to grow in the virtues themselves. But the virtuous life is imperfect also because of the limitations of human virtue as such: when we speak of supernatural virtue we mean the power of God active in the soul, but the use we make of the power is determined by human reason and circumscribed by its weakness; there is a lack of sureness of touch, and a niggling and pedestrian dependence upon rational argument, which you find gloriously superseded in the care-free spontaneity and uncalculating magnificence of gesture of the saints. It is that they are become, in truth, as little children, because they have learnt how the human reason may be perfected by the divine: they have learnt how to judge instinctively with the eyes of God by living in the life of God; they have learnt that to be fully free you must become wholly obedient to the touch of the Spirit.

Always, then, in the christian life there are these two aspects, the man and the child; and it is the child-aspect which makes virtue christian, and which gives to the christian who is possessed of it the freedom and gaiety, the trustingness, the complete absence of self-righteousness and of calculating worry, and consequently the freshness and simplicity, that you find so prominent in the personality of the saint.

There are thus two dangers to be avoided. In the first place, there can be no deliberate cult of childish immaturity of mind and character. There is room in the Church for the "little ones," for those who are naturally simple, unlettered, uncritical; indeed yes; but there is no excuse for a deliberate stunting of gifts of mind and character which God has given. You have to become a personality, to have a mind and will of your own; you have to learn to see and then to judge, you have to acquire the wisdom of the serpent as well as the simplicity of the dove. But then, in the second place, you have to preserve precisely that simplicity; you have to avoid the self-willed piety, the determination to decide at all costs for yourself what is right and wrong, the idea of the virtuous man as the self-made man, which turn virtue from worship of God into something very like worship of the self. You must be able to listen with child-like simplicity to the voice of God and identify your own will with His; then you need the strength and maturity of the grown man in order to make your obedience to the voice not the obedience of a slave or an automaton but the creative gift of a lover.

To learn to be fully man is hard, because it implies all the hardship of asceticism, the constant day by day struggle with what is weakly self-indulgent and disintegrating. But it is harder, perhaps, to learn to be re-born and be a child: to learn first to see and love, to receive life from God instead of trying to make it for yourself, and so to be able to say " I live, now not I but Christ liveth in me." Yet that is the essential. Christian virtue is a question not so much of doing as of being. When you hear it said of someone " He's a different man since he fell in love " you have a clue to what must happen to the christian. As you are, so you will act; love affects one's being, and therefore, in consequence, one's behaviour—even though you do the same things you will do them entirely differently—and it is when you can say " I live now not I " that you can go on to say " I can *do* all things "; and you can say the latter because you add, with the docility of the child, " in Him who strengtheneth me."

Worship, then, is not a part of the christian life: it is the christian life. We shall be thinking, in some of these meditations, of the nature of sin: it is precisely the negation of the child. It is the attempt at autonomy, the desire to be self-sufficient, and to make the self the centre of all things.* And in consequence the wages of sin is loneliness, which is death. For we are not made to be alone, but to live in the fullness of God's life and therefore in the warmth of God's family: it is sin that keeps us apart and closes our eyes. First you must learn to see how your life is meant to be lived: in God, in oneness with all creation: all the things that God has made are made ultimately of the same stuff, so that there is a bond between them like the blood-tie that

*Children can, of course, in their own way, be extremely self-assertive: we are born in sin. The purpose of the contrast here made is not to idealise children in defiance of the facts, but simply to recall what our Lord tells us plainly: there is about childhood a quality which is too often lost in later life, but which we must recover by His grace if we are to be of His Kingdom. It is with this quality that we are here concerned.

binds the members of a family; all the things that God has made have ultimately the same end, to worship and praise Him in their different ways; most important of all, God Himself is present in all the things that He has made, and His presence is discernible in them to the eyes of faith and love and worship—and we best assist the song of creation, and recognize our oneness with all things most truly and most fully, when we learn to see them in God and God in them; and then it is to Him that they can lead us.

But to see things thus is to see them not only in a new light but in a new framework: the framework not of time but of eternity. We cannot escape from the former; but we can acquire the latter, the kingdom of heaven. For the pagan poet there must always be in his love of the beauty of things the sense of their transitoriness, the *lacrimae rerum*; for the christian this is secondary. You cannot wholly escape the sadness of beauty's fading, the pain of loss or the pain of parting; but there is a sense in which nothing fades, nothing is lost, everything that is is eternal, in the mind and heart of God. We mourn what is lost to us in the past, we long for what is not yet ours; but the life of God is not in time, in the life of God there is no past or future, there is only the eternal present. A fleeting moment of beauty is always equally present to God, whether it be for us in the long-distant past or yet to come in the remote future. And so, to share in the life of God is, in a sense, to share in that permanence: it is to have, under all the pain that time inflicts, a deep sense of the abidingness of things, because it is to live, with God, in the eternal present.* So it is to be at peace, to have that peace which the world cannot give: to fall in love is not primarily to *have* something new, but

---

* So Bl. Henry Suso, in his *Autobiography*, writes of the detached man: " God has now become all things to him, and all things have become, as it were, God to him, for all things present themselves to him now in the manner in which they are in God, and yet they remain each one what it is in its natural essence." And later: " Be steadfast, and never rest content until thou hast obtained the now of eternity as thy present possession in this life, so far as this is possible to human infirmity."

to *be* something new : this joy that I have, the actual presence, the sight and hearing, these can be taken from me;
but if all my love is part of my love of God, then the joy
that I am, the joy that can become as it were a part of me,
that must abide, and distance cannot affect it.*

All this should give us a deep realization of the importance of each successive moment, since it is thus in this
sense an eternal moment—an eternal act either of worship
and gratitude and love or of selfishness and blindness. For
ever and ever the priest and the levite pass by the wounded
man; for ever and ever there is the glory of the love of the
good Samaritan; and every moment in our time-sequence
must be either the one or the other.

"Lord that I may *see*!" We have to know and love God
before we can serve Him, with the service not of pride but
of love. We have to learn to see and love the world of all
created things as a family before we can treat is as a family.
We have to learn to think of things not just as things that
we have but as things that we are, if we live in love with
them. The beatitudes tell us how to acquire this life, the
more abundant life which it was Christ's mission to bring
to us, the life of the man who is also a child, the human
life which is also the shared life of God.

The life and power are offered; but we do not acquire
them by passively waiting, but by the hard work of
obedience and prayer. So, as we think over each of the
beatitudes in turn we shall think also both of the sacraments
which bring us the different kinds of energy that we need,
and of the attitude required of us if the energy is to be used
—an attitude expressed on the one hand by the gifts of the
Holy Ghost and on the other by the various types of prayer.

"Send forth thy Spirit and they shall be created," re-
created in the new life. That is the first thing we must think
of : our need of the docility and the selflessness of the
adoring child, rapt in God its Father. To live in the present
is to live in the Presence : to see Him in all things and to see

* I have tried to deal more fully with this in *The Heart of Man*, chap. 1.

all things, all situations, all moments, all interests and desires, in Him. Sometimes we can persuade ourselves that we do this: we think we make Him free of the whole of our lives, when in reality we are keeping some part of it locked away out of sight because we are afraid, because we know that until it is radically altered we can never see Him in it nor it in Him, and we resent the thought of his interference. But as we cannot say we love humanity so long as there are some who are our enemies, so we cannot say we love and worship God as we should until everything we do and are is an act of worship and everything we love we love in His presence.

God made us to know and love and serve Him and be happy. The more you learn, by repentance and prayer and worship, to know Him the more you will love; the more you love the more you will want to serve; the more you serve the more you will be happy. And if you learn to know the creatures of His hand, not just as things that you can have, but as part of the life that you are, the boundless life of love and worship of Him, then you will love them, too, aright, and you will want to serve them also; you will not be torn and disintegrated by clutching feverishly at the fleeting moment of time, but made whole by your vision of the manifold in the One, your power to see and love all things in the peace of the abiding present; and so your heart will be at rest because it will be filled with the all-inclusive Infinity for which it longs, and even here and now you will be happy with the happiness of those of whom is the kingdom of heaven, for you will have been born again into the more abundant life, and the life will ceaselessly grow within you, until at the end you are fully alive at last, and can fully and finally enter into the joy, the complete unshadowed beatitude, of the eternal day.

CHAPTER III

POVERTY OF SPIRIT

Blessed are the poor in spirit for theirs is the kingdom of heaven
MATT. V. 3.

THERE is a sort of infinity in man, because of his power not only to become in a manner all things, but even, by the gift of God, to become one with the Maker of all things. To have our lives thus infinitely enlarged is to be happy; so that it is of this that the beatitudes tell us. But we must start at the beginning. They are grouped in an ascending order: not that as we progress from one to another we leave behind us those that have gone before—all of them are always valid, always necessary—but that unless we can succeed in achieving the earlier we shall never achieve the later. If we cannot be right in our attitude to things we shall never be right in our attitude to anything.

Man is made to be filled to infinity. But for that he must walk as a child with God, he must be able to receive His life, he must know and love and serve Him; and all this is made difficult, and without God's restoring power impossible, because of the fact of sin.

Sin destroys the child. Instead of the docility which makes love and therefore oneness possible, there is the pride of attempted autonomy, the will to be one's own master, which is the state of isolation from God. Isolation from God's family follows. For the proud man who sets out to be master of the world can never love the world; you have the kingdom not of the God of love but of Mammon; you have, not the oneness of knowing and loving and serving, but the chaos which follows from attempting to treat all things as your own creatures, as utilities merely, and to use all things, and animals and men and even God Himself, simply as means to your own profit or pleasure. So you have the man who possesses all things but has nothing; and he has nothing because he is alone, isolated from God, isolated even from God's creatures. What does it profit a man to gain the whole world and yet remain thus estranged, imprisoned, frozen in the husk of his own self-hood? To live the life of Mammon is to be in hell—for hell, like heaven, in the most important sense is not so much where you go as what you become, even in this life it is to be bereft of God.

The first step on the road to happiness is the escape from Mammon. Happy are the poor in spirit. I lose God, I lose the world, I lose myself, if I want only to clutch at things and use them for my own pleasure or profit. So I must, through God's mercy, repent, turn back again, be re-born. I must be "stripped of all things." I must learn the lesson of detachment.

Perhaps few things are more misunderstood than this idea of detachment. People sometimes think that it means not caring: it does, but, as we have seen, only if you add that it means caring too. The detached man will care more for things than the avaricious and rapacious man; but he will care in a different way. He will not clutch and cling, in self-worship; his possessions, his desires, his attachments, will not fetter his freedom and destroy his power of love, will not forever be an anxiety and an agitation of spirit. His is the prayer of the poet,

> "Teach us to care and not to care.
> Teach us to sit still"

and so he learns to be at peace.

The first thing is to care : it is precisely what the rapacious man does not do. We cannot help wanting things; it is our nature; but what makes the difference is how we want, and how we express our want. Things are not just means; they are God's handiwork, lovely in themselves, therefore, and to be treated with reverence. And they are one with us in the unity of God's family; and so they are to be treated with love. And they are His creatures and not ours, and so they are to be used or enjoyed—they are to become possessions— only within the framework of His will. You do no harm to God or to things or to yourself if you use them or enjoy them according to their nature and His will for you, provided your attitude is one of love and reverence, provided you have first learnt to see and love and serve, provided you have learnt to care. We lose the power to love and enjoy things as we should when we lose the power of vision; and we lose the power of vision when we lose the life of the child. When the visionary gleam fades into the light of common day we go on using things because we understand their utility, but more and more we forget that they are things in themselves, things of beauty; we forget to stop and look. But that is just what we must learn again to do: to stop and look. We must learn to stop and look at all the things that God has made that come our way, and say "How lovely you are"; but we must learn to say it as men living not in time only, but in the eternal present, not simply loving the things themselves, but with them praising the God of whom they tell, conscious of their abidingness in His unchanging eternity, and conscious, too, not only that their beauty is a reflection of His infinite Beauty, but that the invisible Beauty is within them and about them, hallowing them : *vere locus iste sanctus est,* truly this world is a holy place since the Holy has made it His home. It is that constant deep sense of the Presence that, if we can acquire it, will prevent our love of God's creatures from distracting us from God. But we must learn, too, to see this inward beauty and holiness in the poor things, and ugly, and the things of mean repute, in the waifs and strays of the world, in the dull and colourless moments as well as in the moments of great joy. And we must learn to see each thing, each event, each fleeting moment, as for ever abiding in the arms of God in the eternal present if we would learn to see them aright; for it is only thus that, to speak properly, we can learn to care.

But then if you care like this you learn also not to care. If you learn to see God in all things you will learn to love them according to His will, not your own self-will. If you see things as in eternity you are less a prey to the pain of their passing, and so you can learn the more easily not to clutch at them as they pass. If you see God in all things and all things in God you learn to be reverent and not proudly possessive. And where it is a question of legitimate possession and legitimate use—and these are measured by the end that God has set for you, your manner of life and the work you do and the needs of your *being*—then you will learn the more easily not to sin by excess or superfluity, nor to hold fast at all costs when God would take from you what He has given : you will learn the more easily not to care.

Let us think a little of the ways in which this caring and not caring is to be expressed. There is, of course, to begin with, the vice of avarice : there is the desire simply to amass as much as one can for one's own ends, and to let nothing go. That way lies complete slavery. But in smaller ways the same spirit can be discerned : the grudging lender, the man who covets and envies, the man who is proprietary about such things as he has, and ungenerous to the needs of others. To be poor in spirit is to be large-hearted and open-handed, to be not too much exercised about legitimate worldly purposes, to be, on the contrary, carefree about success or failure, because whichever it is it comes from God. To be poor in spirit is to have a childlike trust in Providence, and so to be freed from fear.

This freedom from fear is indeed the characteristic of those who have learnt to care and not to care. To be grasping and possessive is to live always in anxiety and fear of loss; to live in the eternal present is to live in the love that drives out fear. *Nihil me separabit*—nothing can separate us from love if love is not what we have but what we are. The poet's paradox ceases to be paradoxical if you see the

different sense of the two words. Teach us to care : teach us
the meaning of love. Teach us not to care : teach us not to
worry, teach us to be free of the fetters of a false love, false
precisely because it thinks of loving in terms of a fleeting
possession instead of an abiding life and oneness. St.
Dominic on his deathbed said to his followers " Possess
poverty." It is not, if you understand it and practise it
aright, a privation; but a perfection, the perfection of freedom. It is not, if you understand it aright, a question
primarily of much or little : quantity is determined by the
end in view. It is a question less of what you possess than
of how you possess it. The apostle must be free of
possessions in the literal sense because he must be free to be
uprooted at a moment's notice at the call of his work : he
must be able to travel light, and light-heartedly; it was that,
no doubt, that St. Dominic had first in mind. But the mere
absence of chattels is not enough : you can be lacking in
poverty of spirit if you possess nothing more than a cloak
or a book; you can be poor even though you possess an
empire if, while saying " all things are mine " you add
" and I am Christ's, and Christ is God's."

Again, you can have few material possessions, perhaps
none, and no avarice of mind about them, and still be lacking in poverty of spirit. You must be care-free about *everything* that you have, material or otherwise. All the gifts
that God gives us are things for which we must care and
yet not care; we are only stewards. You have your own
particular gifts and talents, of body and mind and heart :
you must be open-handed with them, use them in your love
and service of the world, and use them *as* God's gifts to
you, so that you do not mind if what He has given He
should take away : it is not your business, you are only a
steward. You have the gifts He gives you to fill your heart
and your worship of Him : the love He gives you for
others, and the love He gives others for you; these, too,
you must make part of your worship, and part of your love
of His whole family : you are only a steward. You have

the gifts He gives you of prayer and virtue, the help He gives you to climb the scale of perfection : and here, too, you must not grasp and worry and keep your eyes fixed always on yourself; you must do what you can at the present moment to make of these gifts a more perfect worship, leaving to Him the question of progress or failure : you are only a steward.

You are only a steward of all that you have and all that you are; a steward for God and His family. But you are meant to be more than stewards of God's things : you are meant to be lovers as well. If you hurt anything of the things that God has made—by lust, or tyranny, or blindness, or by using things in any way as mere means to your pleasure or profit—you hurt yourself and all the world, because to that extent you continue to destroy the unity of the family. But if you love, and therefore can serve as well as use, can reverence as well as master; if you are a contemplative and have learnt to see and love instead of grabbing, and if your love is worship of God and not of yourself, if your love is as deep as the sea but as care-free as the wind, then you return to the integrity of God's family, and, having nothing, you are at peace, because you have nothing to lose, and at the same time you possess all things, for yours is the kingdom.

Yours is the kingdom of heaven : even in this life it can be true. The desire to have lies deep in us—we are indeed compact of desire—but it is a desire for infinity, which the gaining of the whole world will not fulfil. The desire to have is deep in us : but it is really a misunderstanding if we think of it thus instead of as a desire to *be*. The heart is an infinite capacity and thirst for *being* : and we are never at rest until it is filled. And so we try to fill it by drawing many things towards us and making them ours, till the house is cluttered with furniture, and we cannot move, and still we are tormented. Blessed are the poor in spirit because they have seen that this is not the way, and have known that an infinity not of having but of being is the kingdom. See the immensity, even in this life, of the saints; who having nothing, having no riches, no worldly power or influence, can yet draw all things to them not by force or fear but in love and homage, and so are filled: theirs is the kingdom which has no boundaries, theirs is the earth and sky and stars, and, still more, the uncharted splendours of the light inaccessible; for they have learnt what Mary learnt, and have chosen with her the better part; and it shall not be taken from them.

A.　DEVOTION AND THE GIFT OF FEAR

You shall know the truth : and the truth shall make you free. . . . I will not now call you servants . . . But I have called you friends. You are my friends if you do the things that I command you.

JOHN VIII. 3 ; XV. 15, 16.

If you are poor in spirit you learn not to care, in the sense of not endlessly fretting and worrying, even about your own state of soul. We, in this country and century, are perhaps inclined to take a too negative view of morality: to think it means just not doing things which are forbidden. "Nanny, go and see what Richard is doing and tell him to stop it": that is the voice of morality as we sometimes conceive it; it is not the voice of christian morality. Morality for the christian is religion; and religion is love; and love is not a negative but a creative thing. To know and love and serve: the moral life is a question first of what we ought to be, and only then, in consequence, of what we ought to do—and only thirdly, by implication, of what we ought not to do.

The negative attitude of mind leads us away from the religion of love to the religion of servile fear. What a terrible thing it is to teach the young that being a good catholic simply means avoiding doing certain things, and that if they fail to avoid these things God will see them and will

visit His anger on them. What a different story the gospels
have to tell us. God is love: how can we depict Him as a
sort of omniscient policeman? There is punishment, yes;
but not arbitrary punishment: if I act thus I make myself
thus; and to be thus is itself a misery, a punishment. We
cannot fall into grave sin unawares; we can only go to hell
if we choose deliberately to love evil instead of God, and
therefore become incapable of living any life but the life of
isolation from God, the life of hell.

God is terrible, yes; He is also lovely. You cannot think
of Him aright unless you have both these qualities in mind.
There are times when we have to think of the terror and
the punishment in order to keep ourselves from disaster; but
it means that love and therefore religion are at a low ebb
within us. Servile fear is the lowest motive; there are better
ways of keeping the commandments than that. You could
think of them as what, in fact, they are: the pattern you
have to follow if you want to be whole and happy, a complete human being: that is better than the morality of the
slave. You could think of them also as God's will, the will
of His love, and therefore as religion, as your worship of
Him: the result of living in love, in the eternal present;
and this is the christian way in its fullness; because in this
way you have made your will identical with God's will, and
so you are become one with Him.

But though this oneness is far from the religion of servile
fear, fear of another sort is still an essential element in it.
It is fear which is the beginning of wisdom: without it we
cannot be taught, we cannot grow; but it is not present only
at the beginning. Beyond the completely servile fear of the
slave there is the fear of the loving but as yet unreasoning
child, and its fear is an element we cannot ignore or try to
eliminate, though if we teach and train aright it will pass as
the child grows in grace and wisdom into the higher, freer
and reasoned obedience of the son, in which it becomes
mainly or exclusively reverential. Beyond this again there
is the fear, wholly identified now with loving awe, which is

proper to the lover. The life of the spirit must follow these progressive steps from fear to fear. We shall never learn to love God aright unless we have learnt to sense His majesty, to know Him as terrible. But that same sense of awe is never left behind: it grows as wisdom grows. For it is simply the recognition of the abyss which lies between creature and Creator; and it must grow in intensity as we come to realize more fully what infinity means. This fear, which is not only compatible with but an essential element in our divine sonship, is the *condition* of love as of wisdom; for it is what makes us teachable; and so we have to guard it and labour to deepen and intensify it, till it can become, in the end, a part of heaven's unending hymn of praise and glory.

Surely it is this idea of reverential awe as an element *in* the religion of love that we should teach the young, and not the negative religion of fear alone? But if we are to avoid this unchristian cult of negative fear it will mean that though of course the whole school life must be presented as part of religion, religious practice itself will be as far as possible differentiated from ordinary school discipline and its sanctions; it will mean, too, a very clear distinction between giving guidance and encouragement on the one hand —little children need to be led by the hand to their prayers and confessions, and so on—and anything like enforced piety or dragooning on the other. It means that though you can no doubt preserve them for a time from doing wrong by treating them like hot-house plants, guarding them from knowledge of evil, keeping them in negative innocence, you will not do so: you will not purchase innocence at the price of ignorance and lack of self-reliance. You will want them to know and love and serve God, and so you will teach them the lessons of freedom and responsibility: you will teach them, not to avoid danger at all costs, but to be strong enough to meet and conquer danger: you will teach them, not to want, above all, to be safe, but to want, above all, to love and serve.

God is terrible; we cease to be religious at all if we forget that, and turn Him into a mascot. To grow in wisdom and love is not to lose all fear of God; it is to change our fear of God. It is to pass from the servile fear of the slave, the fear of punishment, to the loving reverence of the son, fearing to offend his father, and in the end to the purely selfless fear of the lover, the fear of hurting what you love. That fear, *reverentia,* remains even in heaven; for it is an essential element in love, in the child-vision; it is also an essential element in art. Without it you can never learn to know and to love; neither can you learn the art of serving God and the world.

But we misunderstand this fear completely if we think of it as endless agitation, anxiety and fright. " Fear not," our Lord says again and again in the Gospel; and if you are poor in spirit how can you fear, since all that you have and all that you are you put into God's hands, secure in trust? If you are filled with the caring which is love and emptied of the care which is worry, then necessarily you are filled with the fear which is awe, but emptied of the fear which is anxiety and fright.

Do not worry. There is a danger for us, in the west, with our latin heritage of logic and law, of falling a prey to the disease of scrupulosity, a disease for which the eastern Church, with its emphasis on grace and freedom, has no name. We must not attempt to lessen our respect for our heritage on this account; on the contrary; but we must make sure that we are learning to see and love the law of God in terms of the life of God, and the clear-cut definitions and directives of ethics in terms of freedom of the sons of God. Our Lord came primarily not to bring us an ethical code, but to bring us life. We cannot have too delicate and reverent an obedience to His will; and at the beginning we necessarily find that we have to force ourselves to obey, and that our motive is often the motive of fear rather than of selfless love; but unless we are trying to turn our obedience, slowly and gradually, into the obedience of love and there-

fore of free choice we may find ourselves being swamped by
negations, a prey to fears and scruples, and in the end become victims of that self-centredness which is the precise
purpose of the Christ-life within us to uproot.

Do not worry. You have to make your examination of
conscience, for example; but let it be, not anxious, meticu-
lous, wholly negative, but sane and brief and positive, the
eye always on love, for it is by love that we shall be judged
in the end. Do not worry. You have, or will have, your
real problems to face: and you must face them squarely,
think them out as best you can, pray and take advice, docile
to God and His representatives; but then, when a decision
is reached, you must rest in God, leave it to Him, refuse
to keep going over and over the same ground, refuse to
become introspective, and set yourself, instead, to the positive tasks of life, be outward-turning in love of God and
His family, be active and creative in the work He has given
you to do.

Be outward-turning: it is the only way to escape from
the bondage of the original sin of self-worship. But be
outward-turning first of all to God.* And what is the first
Godward step, the first step in the life of prayer? Surely
we do well to remember that here, too, "fear is the beginning of wisdom," and that our prayer will be sound and
humble and fruitful if it is built on the foundation of awe.
The first prayer is the prayer of awe of the Unknown, the
prayer of the little child in the face of mystery and infinity,
the prayer of Thomas the Apostle abashed by the response
to his lack of faith: "My Lord and My God." That is the
first prayer; God can begin to do something with us then.
We are taught to say "Our Father"; we are told that

---

* To be outward-turning in this sense means only that we fix our eyes
on something other than our own self, we cease to be self-centred. It
does not mean an absence of recollection; it does not mean anything
other than what Augustine meant when he told us *Noli foras ire*—do not go
out beyond the mind, for God is within the mind. These spatial meta-
phors must be used with caution: the one essential thing, quite simply,
is that we should look at God, not for ever at ourselves.

we are God's family; but we must have not the proud
familiarity which is a form of contempt but the humble
familiarity of the child. Perhaps to achieve it we need a
deep sense of sin; certainly we shall never have it until we
are possessed by a sense of the distance between the Perfect
and the imperfect, the Creator and the creature, between
Being and nothingness; we shall never have it until we can
pray the prayer of awe.

But if we can so pray, acknowledging fully the authority
and the majesty as well as the nearness of God's fatherhood,
acknowledging the abyss into which our sin has plunged us,
and looking in sorrow and humility to God for our deliverance, then we can indeed become His sons, and co-heirs with
Christ, and so be free and happy and at peace.

And what is the gift which can teach us all this? *Initium
sapientiae timor Domini*: we keep our lives and our conduct worshipful first of all by obeying the impulse of the
Spirit through the gift of fear; for so we begin to turn our
backs on what is self-willed and self-determined, we begin
to acknowledge the divine Fatherhood in all that we are
and do, we learn to be docile, we learn to be born again
as little children, and so to become truly wise. The gifts
are all of them forms of docility to the Spirit; but the gift
of fear is the first gift in ascending order precisely because
fear is the first stage in complete docility to the impulses of
the Spirit, and therefore it is what makes it possible for
the Spirit to perfect us wholly through the other gifts; it is
the gift of fear, just as it is that poverty of spirit which is
the corresponding beatitude, which begins in us the reversal
of pride and self-will; it is fear and poverty of spirit alike
which teach us to pray the prayer of awe, and so to begin
our life where it must be begun, in an attitude of reverent
adoration of God.

And to be filled with poverty of spirit and with this fear
which is not only compatible with love but grows stronger
and deeper with the growth of love : this is to become free
of the religion of negations and to begin the life of devotion,

the life in which morality is transformed into worship by the alchemy of love.

The word " devotion," in its turn, is sadly misunderstood in these days. Essentially it has nothing whatever to do with emotion : it is not a question of feeling good. You can be filled with devotion and yet experience nothing but aridity, even an agony of boredom, in prayer. This identification of a loving state of soul with pleasant feelings is very dangerous : you may think you are worshipping God when in reality you are indulging your own desire for a sense of security, your desire to be comfortable and at rest. There are times when God makes the life of prayer very pleasant to His servants; that is His affair, not theirs. The testing time, and the time, therefore, when fidelity to prayer and the life of virtue is most valuable, is the time when nothing is made easy for us, and when we cling on if at all only by sheer strength of will. It is just this, the will, that is the essence of devotion : " the will," St. Thomas says, " to give oneself readily to the things which concern the worship of God." And love, he tells us, is what causes devotion, because it is love that makes us eager to serve the one we love; while on the other hand it is devotion that nourishes love because love is safeguarded and increased by loving deeds, which are the expression of the loving will. And what is it in terms of prayer that causes devotion? It is filling the mind with the thought of God's goodness and man's helplessness : of God's goodness, because this thought brings forth love in us; of our own helplessness, because this excludes presumption, and brings us back again to the humble docility of the child.

" My Lord and my God." The prayer of awe can do two things for us. In the first place it will lay the foundations for our own lives. Learn to live habitually in the thought of the omnipresent majesty of God, the immanent Transcendent : learn to realize habitually that all you see and touch and handle is God's handiwork and still more the habitation of His glory : learn to see every event and action in the light of the eternal present, and every decision you have to make as a decision of love, and the whole tissue of your life as a single prolonged act of worship: learn to say "Our Father" with the thought in your mind that you are a son indeed, but a prodigal son: and then you will be humble and poor in spirit, and be living in the kingdom.

There is the second thing that the gift of fear will do for us. We are all together God's family; you cannot think of your life apart from the lives of these your brothers and sisters. The gift of fear, the prayer of awe, have their social purpose, too. They will help to restore a world living more and more on the surface of life: you must pray, and pray this prayer of awe, to give back the dimension of *depth* to life on earth. William Law speaks of those who try to escape from the terrifying reality of God by seeking refuge in the externals of religion: it is only one stage better than trying to forget reality by the endless pursuit of pleasure. Pray the prayer of awe, and live in docility to the Spirit's gift of loving reverence, and then you will worship in spirit and in truth and help to restore the world to the wholeness of the life of worship: you will help to teach a world proud and uncaring in its belief in its own maturity and its own self-sufficiency that there is no real life, and therefore no real happiness, except in poverty of spirit, except in the infinite life of God: and you will teach all this by being yourself a child, for of such is the kingdom of heaven.

B. THE SACRAMENT OF BAPTISM

Amen, amen I say to thee, unless a man be born again of water and the Spirit, he cannot enter into the kingdom of God.

JOHN III. 5.

The Gospel of our Lord Jesus Christ is the Gospel of life: He came that we might have life, and have it more abundantly. The life and the power are in the world; and the sacraments were instituted by Christ as the normal way in which that life and that power might be poured into our souls. That is why they correspond to all the great crises or turning-points or major needs of life : birth, adolescence, nourishment, marriage (or the special vocation of the priest-hood), sickness, death. They make use of material things, water, oil, bread, because we are not pure spirit but body-spirit, and because not spirit only but the whole material universe needs the restoring power of Christ; they make use of material things also because of the power of material things to speak to the mind and heart of man through sym-bol—and we might think and study and pray a long time before coming to the end of the riches of the Church's symbolism.

The first sacrament is the sacrament of re-birth : pre-cisely the freeing of man from the bondage of the evil power, the mystery of iniquity, in the world, and his re-birth into the kingdom as a child of God, filled, therefore, with the power of God, the power to be good and to do good in the world.

Baptism uses the symbolism of water, and in it you have the two things, the cleansing and the life-giving qualities. " Go forth, unclean spirit," the priest commands : that is the first thing, the liberation from the power of evil; " and give place to the holy Spirit coming down from heaven "; that is the second, the new life. Let us think what exactly this new life means.

First of all you are given truth, wisdom, you are given what we call the Faith. It is not just a series of disconnected statements, to which you are asked to give your assent; it is not only a coherent system of truths about God, so that you know with some accuracy whom and what you are to worship; it is a view of God which essentially implies and teaches a coherent view of life and the world as a whole : you have the key which can unify all your acquired ex-perience and learning, and give a unified direction to all your desires and ambitions. Our civilization tried in the past to order its life and arrange its world-view without reference to God : it wanted to be just human, and to have just a human universe; and now that we are reaping the results we know how miserably it failed. It could not do otherwise. We cannot be just human : we must either accept the gift of God and be more than human, or reject it and become less than human.

But if you have the faith, then you have, first of all, a view of reality which is inclusive, and therefore gives the ultimate answer to the questionings and searchings of the mind : there is nothing too big to become part of it. It satisfies the mind because it enables the mind to see the manifold in terms of the One, which is the perennial need and desire of mind as such.

But it is not just an abstract knowledge of truth that is given in the sacrament of baptism : it is the abiding *presence* of the Truth. God is with us, and in us. And to be faithful to the faith is, therefore, to live always in that presence, and to find in it both the motive force and the standard of judgement for all life and all action. Baptism gives not only truth to the mind, but power to the will. It is a power that must be translated into facility by long and arduous practice, certainly; when we speak of infused virtues we do not mean that we shall begin, as though by magic, to act always and effortlessly in a virtuous way. But we do mean that we are no longer inevitably bound by the bondage of evil to work evil in the world : the seeds of the new life are within us.*

What is essentially given is thus the power of entering into the kingdom, the power of heaven. When the human being is thus filled with the life of God he has within him precisely the life which is heaven, though he has it only

*It is important to make it clear that when we think thus of the power of baptism to bring forth the new life in the christian we are not presuming to limit the power of God in any way : the sacraments are the *normal* means, not the only means ; there is the baptism of desire ; and it is the traditional doctrine of the Church that God does not deny His life and power to any who strive equivalently to worship and serve Him according to the light He has given them : it is not for us to attempt to assess their numbers.

in germ: and all that he does, his thought and willing and prayer and action, can increase that life within him and make him more and more heavenly in himself. Baptism gives us also a new earth; but that is not the thing of first importance. There is no doubt about the mind of Christ here as the Gospels reveal it: the water in the well at Sichar is good and necessary, but not so necessary as the waters of life; the wedding and the wine at Cana are good, but the following scene in the Temple shows us that we must not think the service of God can be subordinated to worldly purposes. If we seek first the kingdom of God and His justice the new earth will be added to us; if we give the earth and its fullness pride of place in our lives and our hearts we are idolaters, and turn the house of God into a den of thieves.

But it remains true that to live the life of God *is,* in fact, to find a new earth, to see the earth as the habitation of His glory, to see all things in Him and Him in all things. We know the power that things have to hurt us or give us joy because of their association with people we love: you love this place because one you love made it heaven for you, you cannot go into this room without pain because one you love once lived in it. To the eye of faith all the things that God has made have this richness of association, and it should always be a cause for rejoicing, because the presence within them is an abiding presence and glory. The pagan *lacrimae rerum,* the pathos of the passing of earthly beauty, is far from being the final word: in the eternal present all things abide, and behind the gleam of created beauty you sense the splendour of the divine. *Vere locus iste sanctus est*: truly this place is holy . . . the house of God and the gate of heaven.

But baptism affects more than our way of *seeing* the world; it gives us not just a new vision of the earth but a new earth. We must see the power of the sacrament in the context of the mystery of iniquity as a whole: the entrance of the power of good into a world given over to the power of evil. This is not simply an affair of the individual soul: it has always its cosmic significance. Think of the history of the world as the history of the struggle between good and evil, the might of God and the might of the rebellious spirit; think of the world as the battleground on which the struggle is waged, and the souls of men as either in bondage to fight on the side of evil or freed to the service of the Light; think of the world of nature as involved in the grip of evil on the universe, and therefore as needing, in degree, the healing and restoring power of the Spirit: and then you will see the significance of baptism for the world as a whole. All that sense, which you find so strongly marked in the early Church, of the power of the God-life in man to heal sickness and suffering and to tame the wild brutality of created things, the power to restore and heal the world by goodness and love, is simply an affirmation of the importance of baptism for the world as a whole. True, the power it gives is primarily a passive power, the power to be a child of God; but that power itself creates a responsibility. You were a slave, now you are free; and therefore you have the responsibility of the free man. You are responsible for your family. You are to share in Christ's healing work: first, of course, for the sin of the world, but then also for its suffering. To be freed from evil is not only to be " made whiter than snow "; it is to become white with the whiteness of white-hot fire, to be on fire to heal and to help. Every christian is meant to be, in Christ, a mediator.

But we shall not mediate as we should, we shall not spread the light in the world, unless we have ourselves first seen the light truly, learnt the true faith and not a travesty of the faith. We believe not in propositions but in the reality which is expressed by the propositions; we believe not in a creed but through a creed. The expression of divine reality in human words is necessarily inadequate; the understanding of the divine reality by the human mind is necessarily groping, and we may well make mistakes. It is possible to accept the formulas of the creeds and still to have

a quite wrong idea of the nature of God and of His providence; it is possible to worship God and still to fall into a
sort of practical idolatry. If you turn your religion into
magic : if you expect an immediate and literal answer to all
your prayers, if you expect the grace of God to do for you
by miracle what only demands a little hard work, you are
misunderstanding the faith. If you think of God in such a
way as to project on to Him the human emotions of
jealousy, anger, spite, you are misunderstanding the faith.
If you turn your worship into self-indulgence, your progress
in virtue into self-glorification or spiritual valetudinarian-
ism, your religion into a purely formal and external affair,
you are misunderstanding your faith. If you allow yourself
to accept the assumptions of a pagan environment as far
as conduct is concerned, and keep your faith in abstraction
from practical affairs, you are betraying it. And you are
betraying it, too, if you think of it simply as something
received from without, a static deposit, which you have only
to accept and guard but without making it your own, without *becoming* it.

The truth is given us from without, yes; but it is something that we have to realize in actual experience : we have
to translate the formulas of the creed into the stuff of life;
we have to learn so to see the faith in all the everyday circumstances and events of life that it becomes not something
we sometimes think of but something we always are. We
shall not mediate as we should, we shall not spread the
light in the world, unless we see the light truly, as it is. But
we shall not mediate as we should, we shall not spread the
power in the world, unless we are sufficiently docile and
humble to receive the truth not with the reason only but
with the depths of the spirit, and so to become really the
instruments of God in and for the world. The christian is
a mediator inasmuch as being one with God he is also one
with his fellowmen, and lives to serve them, to pass on to
them the God-life that is in him : but for that you must be
faithful always to the presence, you must be poor in spirit,

you must have learnt to pray the prayer of awe. Then you will *be* the sort of person who will influence the world, not necessarily by doing much, but simply by being what you are.

That should be the effect of baptism in us : to give us the eternal present beneath and beyond the fleeting world of time, to teach us to live in the presence, and thus to be at peace; to teach us to say "I live, now not I, but Christ liveth in me," and thus to put all things into His keeping. If at long last we can succeed in doing that, we shall know the freedom of the sons of God, the care-free peace that follows upon poverty of spirit and upon the docility of the gift of fear : we shall be gay because we shall not be solicitous, not be grasping, not be self-willed; we shall be gay because we shall be openhearted and openhanded, for we shall know, in the depths of our hearts, that what we are and have is not ours but God's, and shall be glad to know it; we shall be gay with all the new-found gaiety of the child re-born within us, the child who has everything to enjoy and love and nothing to lose; we shall be gay because we shall know that we are no longer in the darkness, that spring has replaced the spirit's winter, the "rains are over and gone," and that if we are faithful we can live not only now but for ever and ever in the Light that is Life everlasting.

CHAPTER IV

MEEKNESS

Blessed are the meek, for they shall possess the land.

MATT. V. 4.

SOME people suppose that to have dominion over great riches and possessions, material and otherwise, is the key to happiness: our Lord tells them that they are wrong, and that, on the contrary, they must be poor in spirit if they want to be happy. Some people suppose that they will be happy if they can dominate their environment, if they are men of power and fulfil their aggressive instinct by expressing to the full what the Gospel calls the pride of life: our Lord tells them that they, too, are wrong, and that to be happy they must learn to be meek.

The second beatitude follows on from the first. You could be poor and still not happy, because you could be poor not from love but from pride, from the arrogance which refuses to share in the blessings of the common herd. Your poverty must go with humility and piety; St. Thomas connects this beatitude, as we shall see, with the gift of piety, for it is the outcome precisely of the sense of our own creatureliness and dependence on God, and in particular of our need of a saviour from the bondage of evil.

There is surely a connection between the superficiality and the arrogance of much of our modern manner of life and thought, and the decay in our times of the sense of sin. We like to think that human nature is capable, of itself, of dealing with the problems which confront it, and of securing its own happiness; and so we fight shy of the deep places with which we cannot in fact deal, and perhaps we pretend that the deepest problems do not really exist at all.

But if we live on the surface of life we miss the meaning of life. There is only one way to know reality fully, and to live fully: we have to die and be re-born.

If you study the mythologies and folk-lore of the peoples of the world—those legends which are either the distorted echoes of primitive revelation or the natural expression of the deepest desires of the heart of man, or both—you find the same theme constantly recurring: the hero must make his long journey through the darkness of the sea or the night, he must slay the dragon or the serpent, he must come through death to the new life, the new birth. And in the christian story which is the fulfilment of these secular dreams of humanity—the fulfilment because in it dream and actual destiny are one—you find the same theme in its highest form in the sacrificial death of the Word who was made flesh and dwelt amongst us that we might be re-born to be the sons of God. But this is not simply a vicarious redemption in which we have no part: what was done in and by Christ must be done also in a different fashion in and by ourselves; in us too the dragon must be slain, and we too must pass through death to the new life. What is the dragon? The power of evil, the mystery of iniquity under whose bondage we are as long as we are living not in God but in sin. And what is the death? The death of the false self, the self set up in rebellion against God, the self which seeks to be self-sufficient. How then are we to be re-born and become whole? By finding our true centre which is God, finding God in all things, and the desire of God in all desires, and so beginning to live the life of worship instead of the life of self-worship. But this in its turn implies a precedent turning away from the false self, an acknowledgement of our essential insufficiency; and, because of our state of sin, an acknowledgement of our need of a saviour without whom we cannot, in our bondage, turn away from ourselves. We find God through making for ourselves the long sea-journey—in the company and in the power of Him who made it for us first; we find God through overcoming, again in His power, the dark evil within us; we find God by realizing in the first place our need of God as a child realizes its need of a father, we find Him by learning to see the reality of sin and therefore to repent and be meek and humble of heart.

"He descended into hell." That, too, we have to do in company with Him. We are all together God's family; and we have to go down into the depths and understand the reality of the evil of the world if we are to help to heal the world. You cannot heal unless you love; but you cannot love unless you see. That is why the first prayer of the humble man is the prayer of the blind man in the Gospel: "Lord, that I may see." Lord, that I may see the reality of sin and my share in it, and so turn again to You, and so see Your mercy and the meaning of the Love that rules the sun and the other stars; for then the Word will be made flesh in me and I shall be re-born, and in the power of the new life I shall share in the work of Him who makes all things new.

You cannot help the world in its sin and its suffering unless you sense your share in the sin and have your share in the suffering. And how can you do this, not only for a few who are dear to you and for whom you are responsible, but for the whole world? You can do it only by putting on Christ, by being able to say "I live, now not I, but Christ liveth in me." And who can begin to say this but the meek and the humble of heart? For the proud man lives aloof, and in isolation, never in oneness with the Life. If you are humble enough to put on Christ, then you begin to live and work in the power of Christ, and according to the will of Christ: you begin gradually to become, in the words of Gregory Nazianzen describing the effect of the Spirit's gifts, *organum pulsatum a Spiritu sancto,* an organ played on by the holy Spirit: you begin to have the obedience and docility to use all your energy in the service not of selfishness but of the Other; to sow, and to leave it to God to do the reaping;

to live in the present, and leave the future issue to His good pleasure.

To be meek, then, is first of all to be obedient: to be obedient, as far as you can, with the loving obedience which is the expression of an identity of will like the identity of the deep personal will between lovers. That is the obedience which is the highest form of freedom, the freedom of the sons of God; and it is thus that we should think of our obedience to the Church, to our vocation, to our conscience: an obedience which sometimes implies a struggle within the mind, sometimes demands much labour and care, but always ends in tranquillity and peace, because there is no agitation, no worry, when once the decision is made or the ruling accepted; for the resulting action is seen in the context of the total struggle between good and evil in the world, and therefore as part of the total divine strategy of love: you take always the long view, you live in the present and leave the future to God.

There is the same need of meekness when it is a question not of submitting to authority but of wielding authority. St. Augustine tells superiors that their desire should be rather to be loved than to be feared: whatever the nature of the authority you have, you must use it, not in order to treat other human beings as pawns, but in order to foster and cherish them as human hearts for which you are responsible to God. Every human relationship is an eternal responsibility. And the greater the authority, the greater the number of laws by which it is answerable to God, and therefore the greater the need of obedience. The Pope is with accuracy called the servant of the servants of God. Every human being is unique: you cannot treat men and women as units in a neat scheme without doing violence to them. (Which is why there is something radically wrong with the sort of school in which each boy is precisely little more than a number: regimentation and education are incompatible.) Every human being is unique; and if you are

called upon to exercise authority over human beings,
whether as parent or teacher or employer or ruler or pastor,
the first thing to remember is that the essence of authority
is responsibility to God for those you govern, and that you
will be judged on love; and the second thing is that if you
regiment you destroy because you ignore uniqueness. Let
us add a third thing, for there are some who think that
authority necessarily means the harshness of an unbending
and callous discipline : our Lord said of Himself, " My
yoke is sweet and my burden light "—and it is no business
of ours to try to improve on Christ.*

Whether, then, you are commanding or obeying, you
have to be meek : the desire to dominate must be turned into
the energy that *serves*. You have within you the instinct to
leave the impress of your personality on your environment,
yes; but you can leave it, not in tyranny and violence, but
in love and happiness. Instincts are in themselves neutral :
it is the expression of them that is good or bad. Our business, therefore, is not to attempt to destroy them, but to
attempt to build something of lasting value out of them.
Meekness, like so many of these old christian words, is often
sadly misunderstood and therefore despised; and of course
you will despise the thing if you think it means a lack of
spirit and energy and strength. But it means, on the contrary, the very opposite of these things. It means not false
humility but the strength that can turn all energies to service
of God and the world instead of the self; it means the
strength of the Baptist, defying kings and leading peoples,
but knowing when the Christ comes that " He must increase, I must decrease." It means using all the power and
the gifts that God has given you, and not pretending that
you have not, in fact, been given them; it means, therefore,
having ambitions, having zeal and zest for great works; but

*There are times when you have to be severe, yes; but the saints know
how to make even severity healing and consoling and strengthening by
making it the unambiguous expression of love ; and even those of us
who are far from holiness can save it from bitterness and destructiveness
by keeping a sense of humour.

always behind the power and ambition there is " Thy will be done "; always the ambition is an ambition to serve for love's sake; and always the power is primarily love-power, that inner power of the personality that you find in the saints, and that relies not on externals, not on riches or violence or a great parade, but on the abundance of the divinely given life within the spirit, the life that calls, but calls freely, to the heart. And that is the power that you can wield without fear, because it is a power which is *received*, and received only by the humble who can put on Christ. There is a danger that even the ambition to be a saint may be a self-willed and self-seeking ambition; but not if you have learnt to be meek; for then you labour to the limits of your strength, you struggle to keep the commandments and to grow in love and in prayer, but you are patient with yourself, you leave the results to God, you do as well as you can at each successive moment, but whether or not you progress is a question you leave to Him.

Meekness, then, is poverty of spirit applied to the whole of life, applied to one's self, applied even to the inner life of virtue. To care and not to care : the courage and strength of the love of the saints in spreading abroad in the world the spirit of love; the meekness and humility of the saints in refusing to be upset by attacks upon themselves : these are the two aspects of a single unified life, the life of humility. To care and not to care : humility can love the whole world because it recognizes that the whole world is God's; and it is care-free because it has nothing to lose—not even its own self-respect.

Happy are the meek, for they shall possess the land. It is better, St. Thomas remarks, to possess than merely to in- habit : he sees the former as meaning " secure," an un- anxious, possession, the sort of possession which you know cannot be taken from you; and that is the sort of possession which is not something you have but something you are. There must necessarily be moments when peace seems to be shattered and happiness a thing infinitely remote; but learn to meet even the *lama sabachthani's* of life as our Lord did—" not my will but Thine be done "—and then, in spite of misery at one level of the mind, you will preserve your peace and your joy in the deep places, you will be able to cast your cares upon Him, and to accept in humility whatever He wills to give or to take away, and so you will be able to go on serenely loving and serving the world, and making it happy.

A.   FAMILY LIFE AND THE GIFT OF PIETY

Little children . . . a new commandment I give to you, that you love one another : as I have loved you, that you also love one another.

JOHN XIII. 34.

Piety is another word which has fallen on evil days and lost its proper meaning. You will find nothing of that soft sentimental escapism which the word seems to suggest nowadays if you study its traditional theological sense. St. Thomas speaks of it as a part of justice : it is a question, therefore, of a plain, matter-of-fact duty, something you owe to something else; and the something else is clearly defined. Justice itself is concerned with the exact payment of what you owe; but there are some debts that cannot, of their nature, be exactly repaid : you cannot repay God for all that He gives you, and so you speak of religion rather than of justice in his regard; and you cannot repay the debt you owe parents and fatherland, and so you speak not of justice so much as of *pietas,* of the virtue of piety. This is a question, first of all, of giving due honour, reverence, devotion, to your parents; but it includes the matter-of-fact duty of seeing to their material welfare if they are in need, of caring for them when they are in ill-health, and so on : and, similarly, that part of piety which concerns one's fatherland is again not a question of patriotic emotions but of a real love and a loving service.*

And what is the purpose of the *gift* of piety? St. Thomas tells us that as the virtue leads us to give due reverence and care to our parents, so the gift leads us to feel for God the love that a child feels for its father, according to the words of the *Epistle to the Romans,* " Ye have received the spirit of adoption of sons, whereby you cry Abba, Father." The gift, then, gives us a relationship to God quite different from that implied in the virtue of religion : it is the sense of creatureliness, but with the addition now of the loving trust of the child for its father; it is awe, but with the addition of a sense of the closeness and loving familiarity of the Infinite Father. Religion worships God the Creator and Lord from afar; here we are led—and led without pride or presumption because led precisely as a child—to that intimate relationship with God which the life of the Trinity makes possible : called to be co-heirs with Christ, to share with and through Christ, therefore, in our own different way, in that same life of the Trinity. It is this gift, then, in particular which brings about in us what we saw at the beginning as one of the essentials of the christian life : the re-birth of the child. And it is this gift, also, which helps to bring about in us the corollary of that sonship : the love of the rest of God's family. The gift of piety, St. Thomas tells us, not only offers reverence and service to God, but also to men inasmuch as they belong to God. As a conse-

*The *patria* is still the land where we were born, the soil on which we depend and which is specially ours, the culture and traditions in which we share ; it is still to our own country that we owe the greatest debt, and to which *pietas* properly refers. But as the world becomes, in some ways, more and more a unity, so the scope of *pietas* is enlarged : we owe, in degree, a debt to all the countries from which we benefit materially or culturally, and ultimately to the whole world ; and when we think of other nations in terms not of the political order but of the universality of the Church, present in all lands, then, of course, the national boundaries should sink further into insignificance ; and while we cling to our own culture and traditions and feel a special duty to our own land, we cannot think of political progress except in terms of the good of the world as a whole.

quence, he adds, it leads us to help those who are in distress or misery.

The two things hang together. "If you love Me, keep my commandments"; but the commandments on which all the others depend is the law of love not only of God but of our neighbour. It is no good pretending to revere God as your Father unless you also, in fact, reverence and serve men as your brothers. The latter is, in practice, the criterion of the former.

Every human being is unique. It follows that every human being has some unique gift to give to his family : to his parents and brothers and sisters in the ordinary narrow sense, first of all, and thence to his country and to the world. The small world of the human home is built up of the gifts of each member of it; the larger world without is built up in the same way of the various gifts, economic, political, cultural, religious, of the individual citizens. If we are christians we dismiss once and for all the idea that our business in the world is to serve ourselves and nobody else, to become holy ourselves and pay no attention to anyone else. Society is for man, yes; but there is a sense in which man is for society, too. We need society in order to grow to be fully men; but we need also to *serve* society in order to grow to be fully men. For without that life of service we doom ourselves to selfishness; and that way we shall never achieve wholeness. When, therefore, we are considering what we shall do, whether in great things or in small, we cannot leave out of account the needs of the family; and sometimes it is our duty to give up what would indeed be very good for us if the pressing needs of home or of country demand our service instead. Live your life in the unity of the home first of all : train yourself to think in terms of what will make the home a better and a happier place; and then in your building up of the home think of the needs and well-being of your immediate neighbours, and thence of your country and of the whole world; and so you will necessarily live a life of love, and fulfil that much at least—and it is a great deal—of the law of God.

Let us think briefly of some of the ways in which we offend God by hurting and perhaps destroying the life of the family.

There is first of all anger, and the sins that spring from it: quarrelling and contentions, loud-voiced or contemptuous abuse; these things are easy to recognise and perhaps easy to regret. But there are less obvious forms of the same vice which yet can do immense and perhaps irreparable harm to the family. There are people who are a burden to live with because though they seldom fly into rages they are touchy, choleric, swift to take offence in small ways over small things; there are those who, as Augustine remarks, are in a still less satisfactory state of soul because, though slow to take offence, they are slower also in asking pardon when in fact ill-temper has overcome them, they nurse their injuries and harbour grudges and brood over means of scoring a petty vengeance for a petty or perhaps an imaginary slight. This state of soul is a slow poison; and makes not only the life of the family impossible but equally the life of worship of God: we are told that if we bring a gift to the altar and there remember that our brother has anything against us, we must leave the gift and go first to be reconciled, and only then return and offer it to God. We might meditate here also on the use we make of wit and humour; for these, too, have to be judged in the light of the happiness of the family. Wit is a precious gift; and you must not let it lie fallow for fear of offending through it; but it demands a great delicacy of touch. There are occasions when the winds of wit have to be tempered to the shorn lambs. The same is true of humour, though it is less dangerous: it would be a tragedy to destroy it in you— what, indeed, is more valuable for a family life than this?— but you have to be sure that love shines always through it, as it so easily can. And when you come to the really cutting and mortifying uses of speech—to sarcasm and bitter irony and spite—then you are in a region where sin may easily be very grave. To have the power to spread laughter and gaiety about you is a lovely thing: its abuse is correspondingly hateful. And as with the tongue, so with the whole personality: it is a denial of *pietas* and a destruction of family life to be even in small ways difficult, prickly, unhelpful, aloof; it is a sign of great charity to be consistently the sunshine in the life of your family and in many other people's lives as well. Morality is thus, here as elsewhere, a far from negative thing: piety is not the avoidance of these sins of anger merely, but the positive duty of making others happy. And we should not forget, either, that anger is only one of the opposing vices in this connection: there is its opposite, a complete lack of zeal, an inability to be roused at all, a sort of stolid indifference to what goes on, whether good or ill: there is a proper time for anger, not in the sense of losing one's temper, but in the sense of a zeal to remedy abuses and to replace evil and hatred by love. This indeed is the proper use of the instinct which finds in the vice of anger its destructive expression: the zeal that will attempt great and difficult things, things which demand high-spirited courage and a sort of ruthlessness with oneself if they are to be done at all, for the sake of the family.

There are the vices of envy and jealousy, which still more completely destroy the soul as well as the family. We should think, in this connection, of their minor forms: scandal-mongering and tale-bearing and spiteful gossip—how many characters have been taken away to the accompaniment of the tinkle of tea-cups?—which themselves lead, in the end, to the greater sins, and eventually perhaps to real hatred. We should beware here of unconscious motivations: it is so easy to persuade ourselves that what we say has to be said for the good of the persons concerned, whereas in reality we are only scoring over them or humiliating them. And what is the true use of the instinct here? You find it in St. Thomas's courteously benign explanation of St. Jerome's advice to Laeta about her daughter's education : " Let her have companions that she may learn with them, envy them and be nettled when they are praised." " Envy," he says, " here means that zeal with which we ought to strive to progress with those who are better than we." There is such a thing as holy emulation, though no doubt it is not an easy thing to acquire.

There is the still worse sin of discord : still worse because if it is bad to hurt one of your brothers by destroying love between him and yourself, it is yet more diabolical—more characteristic of the devil—to hurt two or more of your brothers and destroy the love they have for one another. " Six things there are which the Lord hateth . . . and the seventh His soul detesteth, namely, him that soweth discord among brethren."

There are still other ways in which we can fail in piety towards our family. It is important to remind ourselves that deliberate bad manners can be a sin against charity : an indulgence in that sort of vulgarity which, because it is strident, grates upon people's nerves and can cause real distress, or in the type of mannerism which, so far from being a charming or amusing idiosyncrasy, is a trial to those we live with; the priggishness which is a form of pride, and the snobbishness which, because it judges people at best on unessentials, is a form of blindness. There is the sin of ingratitude, and taking other people's devotion or self-sacrifice for granted as our due. There is the sort of isolation which is reserve gone mad : you may be kindly enough disposed inside yourself, but your manner is such that people hesitate a long time before appealing to you for help, because you give the impression that you will not want to be disturbed and put out. This is akin to the vice of " incuriosity " of which St. Thomas treats : and which implies a sort of mental stagnation as far as social life is concerned, a lack of zest and interest which is also a lack of charity and responsibility, and denotes a lost childhood—

the soul grown old and stale. You cannot be living in love and piety if nothing outside yourself has interest for you. On the other hand there is the vice of curiosity: which is the wrong sort of desire for information. It may be wrong because it is proud: you want to know all about people and things because it feeds your sense of power; it may be wrong because it is dissipated, distracting you from more important things; or because it is a form of trespassing, that ruthless inquisitiveness to which nothing is sacred—people sometimes need to be reminded that to read letters not addressed to them may well be a grave sin; it may be wrong because it is directed to scandalmongering and gossip; it will be wrong if in any way it is the expression not of a loving interest in others' lives but of an anti-social inability to mind one's own business. You must preserve or recapture the childlike quality of concern for the family; but always distinguish it from the insatiable flutter-pated inquisitiveness which can never bear to be unacquainted with whatever is going on, however unimportant or however private.

Let us, to end this examination of conscience, consider some of the remaining ways in which, by excess or defect, you can fail to be the sort of person who makes family life what it ought to be, a continual joy. You will fail if you are glum, and never have a word of encouragement or gratitude or praise, or even a word at all, for those around you; on the other hand you will fail if you are garrulous and boring, producing a constant stream of meaningless small talk which swirls about the heads of your relatives until they feel submerged and stifled. There is a point at which untidiness becomes a sin, because it causes real discomfort and inconvenience to others; there is, on the other hand, the finicky tidiness, the passion for quite unnecessary exactitude, which can never bear to see anything a millimetre out of its proper position, and must have every household event timed to the second, and the home itself bound tightly in domestic red tape. You are impious if you are cold and unresponsive; but you are impious also if you gush. It is a

sin to be testy; but there can be also a dangerous lack of
solicitude in that sort of thoughtless and bovine heartiness
which administers heavy slaps on the back at the breakfast
table, or in the loud jocularity which is insensible to the
needs of a quieter mood. Moreover, while it is a horrible
thing to be thinlipped and humourless, it is at least a very
dangerous thing to be a practical joker, and almost certain
to be boring; and these things, if they are hardly to be
classed as sins, at least could be regarded as imperfections.
Similarly, people who are darkly secretive are a pest, and
people who tend to be shocked are a worse one; but indis-
cretion and a complete lack of reticence are not lovely qualities either. Finally, there are people who have to dominate
the household and control whatever is going on, and always
take the centre of the stage; and there are others who have
no spirit and contribute nothing to the common life : and
both types are lacking in piety.

It is important to remind ourselves often that the cultiva-
tion of a right sense of humour can be one of the forms of
piety. Cultivate a sense of humour in yourself about other
people, and in other people about yourself : learn to laugh
rather than be vexed by other people's foibles, but learn the
ability also to let other people laugh at your own. It is not
a virtue to be uncritical; on the contrary; but you have to be
sure that your judgements are not hasty or spiteful, and
that the growth of the power of criticism is accompanied
by a growth in gentleness. Acquire the sort of personality
that people will instinctively take their troubles to : and you
will acquire it by learning to be pious and to love.

This piety towards the family and thence towards the
greater world outside is a virtue; but we need the gift as
well if we are to practise it fully and spontaneously. If you
learn to treat God as your Father you will automatically
come to think of men as your brothers, and to love them as
your brothers precisely in the unity of God's family, so that
your love for them and for Him is one single love. For
piety towards God gives us a constant and inclusive sense

of the *providence* of God : we learn to see every event as His will, and to accept it as such; not, of course, that we have no ambitions, and make no effort to achieve what seems to us to be good, but that whether our efforts meet with success or with failure, and however things fall out over which we have no control, we see in them all the guiding hand of God, and accept them with care-free trust and confidence, since all that we have and are, and all that we want and love and cherish, is secure in the eternal present of His mercy. This is indeed the very essence of the life of religion as opposed to the life of self-will : the growth towards that complete identity of will, that complete abandonment of self to the saving and sustaining arms of God, of which the mystics tell us, and without which we can never learn to care and not to care, and never live in that peace which the world cannot give. There is no such thing as chance : we tend to think too readily in terms of accident and coincidence and fate and " the way things turn out," and so perhaps we miss many an indication of the way our duty lies, and many an opportunity to do service to love. This sense of the pervasive providence of God is a thing we have to learn by constant reference and attention : whatever happens is His will, and has a meaning, and is meant to be of use; whatever happens will be turned eventually to good in His restoring and redemptive power; whatever happens, therefore, I must accept with equanimity in my deepest heart, however sad or tragic it may be, because in Him all things are one, and there is nothing that escapes His providence and lies outside His purposes for the world. Our Father . . . Thy will be done : the two things go together; it is because we say the first that we can hope to mean the second.

All this can come only after a long and arduous effort to be faithful to God's help in all the small events of life; it depends on growth in prayer and courage and patience; but if we can gradually school ourselves to take everything thus with docility and peace from God, we shall at the same time learn to be equable and at peace with men. Piety towards God implies and causes piety towards men. It is not, again, that we must have no ambitions of our own, or make no effort to influence situations and events: far from it; but when, in fact, our efforts are unrewarded, when people are difficult or antagonistic and cause us sorrow, still we shall not be flustered or desperate or hopelessly depressed, because we shall know that this too is in God's hands, and that we must not worry, and we shall go on thinking of mankind as our family.

The life of action is dependent on the life of prayer. If we would have the quality of piety in our lives we must have the quality of piety in our prayer. We must take the prayer of awe a step farther: God remains the *mysterium tremendum* before whom we are as nothing; but He is also our Father; the awed fear of the child in face of the unknown becomes the reverential love of a known person, a Father. "Hallowed be thy name": the Transcendent is near to us because we can name Him; and very near to us because the name is Father, and calls forth from us confidence and trust and love. But it is still the confidence and trust and love of the child.

Piety, then, is a necessary quality of our attitude both to God and to men. And in the last resort the two things become one: for we best acknowledge the fatherhood of God when we acknowledge it in the company of our brothers. We pray best, and we labour best, when we pray and labour as a family. "Wherever two or three are gathered together in My Name. . . ." We should stop sometimes and think, at Mass especially, "I am praying with my family"; for it will colour our attitude to our family. We should think of it sometimes also because zeal is infectious; and if we pray fervently ourselves we may help others, and equally if we pray fervently it may be because we are being helped by others. For the same reasons we should cherish particularly the old tradition of family prayers; for these can sanctify the home as nothing else can, and make it itself a real unity in love, and the family life a real worship of God.

At the end we shall be judged on love. Love of the family, small and great, is the test of our love of God. Our Lord said of Mary the sinner that much was forgiven her because she had loved much: it is a lovely epitaph to be called a great lover of God and of men, and if through our lives we have laboured hard to love and serve those with whom our life has brought us into contact, then of us, surely, He will say at the end that much is forgiven us too, because we have loved Him and shown our love by loving his family.

B.   THE SACRAMENT OF CONFIRMATION

But the Paraclete, the Holy Ghost, whom the Father will send in my name, he shall teach you all things, and suggest unto you all things whatsoever I shall say to you. . . . Let not your heart be troubled, nor fear.

JOHN XIV. 26, 27.

If we are thinking of our duties towards our family and God's it is natural that we should think of the sacrament of confirmation, since it is precisely the sacrament of the social life of the christian, the sacrament which fits him to be a full member of the family.

Let us look first of all at the symbolism. We are meant to see the sacrament as a repetition of the first Whitsuntide: the Paraclete, the Strengthener, comes not indeed as it were in tongues of fire nor to give us the gift of tongues, but with similar energizing and encouraging purpose, to "kindle within us the fire of His love," that we being re-created may be used by Him to renew the face of the earth. It is the sacrament of social action; but social action begins when responsibility begins: when we grow up. It is the sacrament of adolescence. That is when you begin to gain your freedom and independence; when, in consequence, you have to face the greater world and decide whether you are to allow it to mould you or whether you are strong enough, on the contrary, to impress your personality upon it as a responsible man, an artist and creator of new life. The results of this first encounter with a perhaps hostile, perhaps pernicious environment can be so far-reaching, and it is so easy to fail and to be submerged, that you need all the help you can get: you need the strength and the fire of the Spirit to retain your integrity and increase your abundance of life. Confirmation is meant to help us here. But it has also its purely supernatural purpose: it is meant not only to help us meet the particular problems of adolescence but also to make us spiritually mature. The grace is given as *power*; all the symbolism is military symbolism: the anointing with oil for the warrior spirit, the signing on the forehead to drive out fear, the tap on the cheek for the virile bearing of hardships, and the idea of fire, heat, following on the baptismal water, to signify growth.

But what is the purpose of this growth and fire and strength? The reference is always to the family, to the world in need of restoration: the power given is not merely given for our own private sanctification; it is given in order that we may be able to help others to become holy by becoming holy ourselves. You have to *fight* as a soldier— though to fight, let us remember at once, with the weapons of love—and to fight as a soldier means necessarily to fight for somebody else, to fight for a cause.

That is what these qualities are for; that is what the maturity of soul and conscience is for. You cannot fight as you ought in the age-long struggle between good and evil unless you know what the struggle is about; you cannot fight as you ought unless you have initiative and can bear responsibility; you cannot fight as you ought unless you are strong enough to accept dangers and hardships lightheartedly and not be dismayed.

Confirmation is the sacrament of social action. You are

meant, through the power it confers, to be able henceforth
to contribute actively and creatively to the family life of
the Church and of the world. You must be meek and pious;
but that does not mean being a blind fool waiting for an
order before you can move, lost and panic-stricken as soon as
you are left to yourself. You must be obedient to the authority of the Church; but it is the obedience of the free man
that is demanded of you. You cannot expect a direct inspiration from God or a direct lead from His representatives
on earth in every little event and circumstance of life : it is
part of your duty, as a mature christian, to be able to apply
for yourself the things you believe about God to the things
you have to do among men.

Confirmation is the sacrament of the common priesthood
of the laity : every christian is meant to share in degree in the
priesthood of Christ, as we shall see in detail later on;* every
christian is called to be with Christ as mediator, to help in
the redemptive work of Christ in the world, to lead the
world back to love through love. And that means that he
must have knowledge and bravery and initiative and per-
severing strength; but it means that they must be gifts received, they must be the fruit of docility to the Spirit. It is
the meek who, possessing the land, can sanctify and sweeten
the land; it is those who obey the Spirit through the gift of
piety who can give a full and creative service to the family;
it is those who have filled their hearts with the sense of
God's continuous care and providence, and so have identified their wills with His, and can live with a carefree abandon to His good pleasure, who can do in the world the will
of the Father in union with the Son.

When you think of the christian duty of social action,
when you think of the apostolate of the laity, think first of
all of the upper room in which the timorous apostles were
huddled in hiding : it was to these immature souls that the
Spirit came, and through them that the Spirit worked to
such effect that their "sound went forth into the whole

*Cf. infra., pp. 169 sqq.

world, and their words to the ends of the world." You must fight for the cause of love with the weapons of love, for the cause of poverty of spirit and meekness with poor and humble means. There is something a little suspicious about schemes of social action which begin with a grandiose display and a grandiose expenditure, with heavily-embossed notepaper and offices at a smart London address. There may, indeed, be nothing wrong; but at least make sure that behind it all there is what matters most and what alone will do work for God : the selfless zeal and the consuming fire of God-filled men and women. There is always the danger that we may think we can do the work of the Spirit in the world by purely external activity, by being busy about many things, without bothering at all about what we are and what we love. That is why we have thought in such detail of the ways in which we can fail our family, fail in piety. If this is not as it should be, our work for the world will certainly not be what it should be. People are not deceived by an imposing façade for long : they look for the living sub-stance behind the appearances, and the more ambitious the appearances the more they will rightly expect to find behind them; and if we challenge them thus to look and allow them to be disappointed we are doing not the Spirit's work but the devil's. Being is more important than doing. You can be an apostle, you can use to the full the grace of confirma-tion, even though you belong to no society, no social or-ganisation, within the Church : you can be an apostle by being the sort of person whose loving absorption in the presence of God and loving obedience to the will of God is apparent to all who have eyes to see. And on the other hand you will never be an apostle, you will never be faithful to the sacrament, unless you are that, even though you join with zest in every form of catholic action you can find.

Let us be simple about all this, and go back to the simplest things for our pattern. Who is it who really shows *pietas* towards his family, his neighbours, his friends? It is not the man who does a great deal, necessarily; on the contrary, he may be a nuisance, he may intrude, he may poison his service with condescension. Piety must be, first of all, a quality of being: must mean being the sort of person who is felt to be loving and interested and sympathetic and anxious to help when help is required; and the actual carrying out of that will to serve, precisely because it is always the expression of a state of being, and can never be simply a parade, is necessarily a form of piety because it is a form of reverence and love.

The purpose of confirmation is to enable us to help others to be holy by *being* holy ourselves. The primary purpose of Catholic Action is to carry forth into the world a power of a God-filled personality—*organum pulsatum a Spiritu sancto.* If you want to be used by the Spirit in His work in the world there is this one essential preliminary: you must be meek, you must have docility.

The apostolate of reason is always a necessity: there is always need of those who can explain and defend the faith, and state it again in terms which can be understood by the contemporary mind; indeed it may be that now more than ever before this necessity weighs upon us. And yet perhaps it is not the supreme task of today. The world gets very tired of argument. It would be more accurate to say that the labours of reason *alone* are not the supreme task; and that the world gets very tired of argument which it feels to spring only from the head. You need to have a very firm and very clear grasp of the truth, and you need to be able to state it clearly; but if you want people not only to listen politely but to keep your words in their hearts and be changed by them, then you must become, through the power of the Spirit, the sort of person who draws people and disturbs and uproots them without their knowing why, because he is what he is. The supreme task of today is a question of being: because it is a question of bringing back to the world the direct *experience* of the power of love in the world; it is a question of bringing it face to face with the immensity of the Paraclete, the Strengthener, filling and shining through the bodies of men. When you have been shaken to the roots of your being by the mere presence of someone who stands for a truth, then you are impelled to examine the truth he stands for, and predisposed to apprehend it. " Kindle within them the *fire* of Thy love "; then " they shall be re-created, and·Thou shalt renew the face of the earth."

The Holy Ghost comes down at Pentecost upon the christian family : bringing a common power and fire for the common task. That is the best way in which we can work as christians in the world : to be first of all ourselves a family, and then as a family unity to serve the larger family of the world. There is no short cut. You bring your own unique contribution to your home, and help to build up its unity and its charity; then your home, in its turn, helps to build the unity and charity of your country, so that your country, too, if it is faithful to its vocation, may bring its contribution to the life, and help to forge the unity, of the world : that is your task in the kingdom of this world. And in and through that work you have your work for the Church; and it follows the same lines. Through your family life, your family worship, your family prayer, you help to build up the life of your parish and of the whole catholic community in your country, and so eventually of the Church as a whole. And whether you think of this creative work in terms of the home, or the parish, or the country, or the Church, it is always the same thing in the end : love flinging wide the doors to those outside, quietly anxious to heal and help, quietly ready to fulfil the will of God in this life of service, humbly grateful for being allowed to serve.

Because love and hatred are abstract nouns we must not minimize their power. The world is filled with the spirit of evil, with hatred; and it is a real influence in the world, which can be felt as a bleak wind is felt, even though we may not be actually conscious of its effect upon us. But there is love in the world, too, though so little of it in men compared with the world's need : and that, too, has its often unconscious effect on the souls of men; and it is that that we have to increase and intensify as a part, and perhaps the chief part, of our apostolate, and the work of our common priesthood; so that when the faith is mentioned it may suggest more to the non-christian than a system of beliefs, a view of reality: it may recall, primarily, the power which is love-power, the feeling that in the company of Christ's followers there is life and joy and welcome, the feeling that the Church is not an alien and forbidding territory upon which it is unpleasant to trespass, but, on the contrary, a place which seems immediately familiar and tranquillizing, and a place of peace, because immediately you enter it, and without having to look much about you, you realize what you had not realized fully before—that it is home.

CHAPTER V

THEY THAT MOURN

Blessed are they that mourn for they shall be comforted.
MATT. V. 5.

WE have been considering our Lord's reply to those who think of happiness in terms either of possessions or of the proud fulfilment of the aggressive instinct; St. Thomas, when he deals with this third beatitude, explains it in terms of the way in which creatures can be the occasion of our turning from God, if we regard them as the highest good, and in particular of the search for pleasure, the delight and appeasement of the senses. We might perhaps think here of one particular—and perhaps particularly dangerous because insidious—way in which the demands of the senses can exercise a sort of tyranny over us: the search for comfort, not so much in the sense of material self-indulgence, as in the sense of a determination to arrange one's own life pleasantly, to feather one's nest, and then to let nothing and nobody interfere with its quiet and harmonious course. For this can indeed turn a man from God, and become itself his highest good, to which everything else must be sacrificed.

You can be kindly, for example, and even positively kind, so as perhaps to deceive even the elect; but your kindness stops dead at the point at which your nicely-planned mode of life will be interfered with. You can be friendly, and even have a great gift for making friends; but sooner or later it becomes clear that instead of loving your friends you use them. You can be sympathetic, benevolent, patriotic, religious-minded, but always with this reservation: you keep these things in their place, and their place is the carefully allotted place your egotistic scheme of things allows them.

You will not have your comfort invaded at any price. Then you are not in the company of those that mourn; on the contrary you are still in the service of Mammon.

The christian must die in order to be re-born; and the death is the death of the self that sets itself up to be independent: to be a god, and to use all things as its creatures, for profit or pleasure. Here we think, in particular, of the search for pleasure: you will use things, and be quite prepared incidentally to be fond of them, just so long as they fit in with your scheme and minister to your comfort. But that is not the christian attitude. It is on love that the "whole law depends"; and this condescending affection which will use things on conditions is not love. In love every getting is a form of giving; this other attitude is a sort of lust, where every giving is only a form of, or a means to, getting. The centre is yourself; in love the centre is always the other, and yourself only as identified with the other. The pleasure-seeker in this sense is enslaved to the original sin: he has yet to die, to make the long journey and slay the serpent, and find himself anew and truly in the Other. There is no love without reverence; but reverence consists in saying "It is *you* who are important."

Blessed are the meek: you have not left this beatitude behind when you come to the next one; you will not be of the company of those that mourn unless you have learnt to be humble. And humility in this present context is a humility about and towards the things that surround you: you must reverence reality, and so in your use or enjoyment of it you must be temperate—for temperateness, as we shall see, is not the quenching or diluting of passion but the deepening of it: not allowing it to dissipate itself in meandering shallows, or to become isolated from the full personal life, but, on the contrary, making it essentially a part of the wholeness of the body-spirit, and essentially, therefore, a part of the body-spirit's worship of God. Passion cannot be worship of God unless it is reverence towards its immediate earthly object; and just as piety towards creatures is the test of piety towards God, so with reverence. If you want to be among those that mourn you must start by making sure that you are temperate in your attitude to creatures: that you are reverent towards men and women and animals and inanimate things. You must not be sentimental: you must not make reverence synonymous with fear or softness or blindness. There is an order in created things, and the less are meant to serve the greater, and to serve them according to their nature. It is not reverence but irreverence to treat your pets as though they were beings of a superior order: it is a failure to respect their nature. It is not reverence but irreverence to refuse from mistaken humanitarianism to punish a disobedient child. But you can be reverent to the nature and personality of the child you are punishing, though it is a very different reverence from the reverence the child owes to you.

Blessed are the meek, then; because in this question of our attitude to things they have the power to be humble, and therefore to be temperate. But this present beatitude takes us further than that. The gift, St. Thomas points out, goes further than the virtue: and enables us to cast off desire altogether, if need be, or even to choose discomfort and sorrow. You are so far from subordinating everything to your own comfort and well-being that, on the contrary, you subordinate these readily and gladly to the needs of others. You are so far from refusing to have your life invaded that you yourself are always leaving it to give help to others. You are so far from determining to "keep yourself to yourself," you are so far from regarding your own private life as a sacred preserve, that, on the contrary, you have learnt the essential christian lesson that all that you do and all that you are affects the rest of the world, and the rest of the world is your family. You are your brother's keeper.*

*There are, of course, degrees of responsibility. A man is responsible in strict justice for his children, for example ; he cannot have the same obligation towards strangers to whom he is in no way related. The

Let us note at once : they shall be comforted. The quest
of invulnerability, the search for a comfortable life beyond
interference, the refusal to be put out by anything or any-
body : these will bring not comfort but misery, because their
end is isolation and death of soul. You will be undisturbed
if this is your object, oh, yes; and unless you are so dead as
to have no feeling left to you you will cry out for someone,
however uncomfortable, to share your loneliness and your
misery with you. But they that mourn, they shall be comforted; and they shall be comforted, not simply by a sub-
sequent reward, a belated consolation prize for what they
have suffered, but because their sorrow itself will be *turned
into* joy even on earth, the sort of joy that gives life and
strength and courage and exhilaration.

They shall be strengthened. Once again modern use has
debased the language : we think of comfort first of all in
terms of material things—an easy chair, cushions, soft
slippers—and then, when we speak of somebody giving
comfort, of a soothing influence, a smoothing away of cares,
which has something similarly soft about it. These things
have their place, the second one especially, in the idea of
being comforted; but they are secondary. The Paraclete,
the Comforter, is not primarily a soothing influence. The
word itself means a strengthening : it is, if you will, a
soothing influence—this is sometimes a necessity—but only
in order to give renewed courage and strength to face the
reality which has overwhelmed the sufferer. And perhaps
here there is a clue to our Lord's apparent paradox. Blessed
are they who are ready and anxious to go to great lengths,
endure great discomfort, in order to bring strength and
courage to others : for in their giving to others of these
demands of charity, too, have their degrees of urgency. But the lesson
of the Gospel is that there is no human need, and no human evil, which
can leave us entirely unmoved : our love of God and our divine sonship
make us a family ; we each have our share in the responsibilities of the
family as a whole ; and charity must make us feel the need of helping
suffering wherever we meet it, sharing in the penalties of sin wherever
we come across them, and joining at least by our prayer in the general
burden of sin and sorrow in the world.

things they will themselves receive them. To encourage another to great deeds is to be strengthened yourself. And (lest we lose sight of the gentler side of comfort in stressing the stronger) there are few things that bring greater balm and peace to the soul than to bring them to the soul of another—as the confessor knows so well by experience.

But how are we to bring ourselves so to obey the Spirit's promptings as to be able thus to comfort, and, in general, to suffer with, not only the few who are dear to us but the many who are in need? We must go back to the thought of our solidarity in sin; and our duty to share in the redemptive work of Christ. We share in the guilt of the world: we must share in the sufferings for which the guilt is responsible. It is not for us to try to assess our precise measure of guilt; no one can tell that but God. We may not be among the spectacular sinners, but we are not to know that their sins are not less heavy on their souls than our own smaller sins on ours, for we are not to know that grace has not abounded in us immensely more than in them. It is easy to say "He has murdered and I have not; so he is a greater criminal than I"; but no one can say "He has murdered and I have not and therefore he is a greater *sinner* than I." We come back, then, to the sense of sin; for if we really understood the sin that is in us we should not be in any mood to attempt to assess our particular degree of responsibility for the guilt and pain of the world. That is why the sense of personal sin and personal responsibility grows greater as you come nearer to holiness; and that is why the idea of measuring guilt against guilt is in the last resort irrelevant. What Christ did we must try to do: and He, being guiltless, took upon Himself all guilt. We are each, in Him, responsible for all.

But to be responsible is more than to share in guilt and consequent suffering: it is to share in *redemptive* suffering, the sort of suffering that helps to *take away* the sin of the world. Go back to the simple facts of ordinary human sympathy: love is unhappy if it is *not* sharing in the other's pain, but why? Not simply because, through the identity of heart and will, when one suffers the other automatically suffers too, but also because the sharing is felt to be a helping, a strengthening, a comforting. And if you are living in God, and therefore see His family as your family also, you will be impelled to feel thus about all His children: nothing human will be alien to you, and in particular no human cross will be a matter of indifference to you: you will want to share the sufferings of all because you will share God's love for all.

Blessed are they that mourn: but to do that in the Gospel sense you must become the sort of person to whom others spontaneously take their troubles; and there is only one way to do that. *Si vis amari, ama:* you will find others anxious to share their troubles with you if you desire to share them; and you will desire to share them if you love.

Blessed are they that mourn. We should see the Commandments in this light; for while in themselves they state the negative minimum, charity carries them right over to the positive maximum: not only that you must not be intemperate and selfish in your desires, but that you must be ready, if need be, to set aside your desires altogether, and even to choose discomfort and sorrow. It is not enough that you should not do murder: you must be ready to lay down your own life for your brethren. It is not enough that you should not steal: you must be ready to give of your own possessions when your brethren are in need. It is not enough that you should not commit adultery: you must be ready even to give up your own family life and its comforts if God calls you in that way to serve your brethren. It is not enough that you should refrain from covetousness: you must have the positive quality of poverty of spirit. It is not enough that you should not take away your neighbour's name and character: you must be ready, if need be, to become yourself an outcast if love demands it of you. All that divine recklessness which you find in the saints is in this beatitude: being poor in spirit they are not tied down by possessions, being meek they are not held back by self-respect, but being of those who mourn they are yet more fully free, because they want to hold back nothing for themselves—of time or trouble, of ease or security—and so they can give all they have and all they are to their brethren. And they are comforted: they are strengthened and consoled, not when their troubles are over, but in their troubles, because, in the first place, their labours are the labours of love, which is its own reward, and because, in the second place, their sorrows have an instant response of love and gratitude from those they have helped—including God Himself.

There is a third reason. As there is a solidarity in sin so there is a solidarity in atonement. Those who mourn are helping to bring souls to God through their love, through helping them to bear their crosses as Simon of Cyrene helped our Lord. But to take up a cross thus for and with another is to turn it into a tree of life. There are things you will never know, never understand, except through suffering, and especially through suffering *with* another. Knowledge is not perfect until it becomes love-knowledge; and the way to the deepest love-knowledge is through suffering. You cannot know the depths of reality until you have been down to the depths of reality; but you learn most when it is with and for another that you go. And this need not be a conscious sharing between two particular human beings, though this is the easiest way. There is a solidarity in atonement. The most practical application of all that we have been thinking is indeed this: that whatever suffering and sorrow may come to you, and whenever it come, it can be used, and ought to be used, in the power and in the company of Christ for the healing and the comforting of the world as a whole; and in that sharing of the sorrow of the world as a whole you can find your understanding and your heart immeasurably enlarged, enlarged indeed to something remotely approaching the fullness of the stature of Christ.

They shall be comforted. "It is more to be comforted in

the kingdom than merely to have and possess it," says St.
Thomas; " for there are many things the possession of
which is accompanied with sorrow." One of them is love.
But the sorrow that love brings in its train can so easily be
this strengthening and up-building sorrow, the sorrow that
heals and renews; and that sort of sorrow is comforted because it is itself a thing of joy. To lust after more and more
things for the sake of the pleasure they can give; to cling
more and more to things or to a settled and pleasurable way
of life because of the material comfort that is in them : this
is to have more and more care, and more and more loneliness, and therefore more and more sorrow. But to share
more and more deeply in the all-inclusive love and sympathy
and suffering of God is indeed to have sorrows, but to have
sorrows that are turned immediately and inevitably into joy
because they are the stuff of vision and understanding and
love, and in the glory of the vision and the love they glow
with fire.

A.   SINGLE-MINDEDNESS AND THE GIFT OF KNOWLEDGE

For in his hand are both we, and our words, and all wisdom, and the knowledge
and skill of works. For he hath given me the true knowledge of the things that
are : to know the disposition of the whole world, and the virtues of the elements,
the beginning and ending, and the midst of the times.

                                                    WISDOM VII. 16–18.

They that mourn, they who can forget their own desires
altogether if need be, or even choose discomfort and sorrow,
in order to serve Love in all things, they are the ones who
in actual practice achieve wisdom because they have brought
the manifold into unity by seeing God in all things and
turning their love and service of all things into a single act
of worship of the One. St. Thomas associates this beatitude
with the gift of knowledge, because, he says, the gift leads

us to mourn over the way we have allowed creatures to distract us from God: to distract us because we have turned them into a means of comfort or pleasure, and so enjoyed them apart from and in opposition to God.

"He sees God aright who sees Him in all things." The gift of knowledge enables us to judge of everyday things and events from God's point of view: seeing Him in all things, and seeing them, therefore, in the light of the eternal present as His handiwork and His habitation, we judge of them not as though they were our creatures to be used as we please, but as part of our worship of Him. But to do that is at once to dethrone the pleasure-principle, and to accept a standard of judgement, and acquire an attitude of mind, in direct contradiction to it. We are only stewards.

Let us recall, first of all, what sort of a judgement this is. The gifts are given us to correct and supplement our natural powers. There are two ways in which virtues are imperfect in us: first, because we possess them imperfectly; and this imperfection is removed by greater fervour of life, and therefore a more complete possession of the virtuous habits; secondly, because of an inescapable imperfection in the habits themselves: they are God-given, but they have to bow to the limitations of human faculties, of the human reason; and so faith, for example, is in itself obscure, and prudence or temperateness are limited by the ability of the mind to decide what the prudent or the temperate course of action is in any given case; and this second imperfection can only be removed by the presence of a higher habit in the soul: the presence, in fact, of the direct impulse and guidance of the Spirit. When we speak, then, of the gift of knowledge, we leave far behind us the mental ability which comes of book-learning or the analysis of experience by a keen intellect: we are in the realm of the wisdom which comes direct from God, and which you are likely to find in the unlettered and simple more often perhaps than in the brilliant and the learned, since it is the fruit of the soul's docility to God. When you find a poor peasant woman, unable to read or write or understand abstruse matters, but startling you by the deep penetration and the sureness of touch with which she judges human affairs and motives and duties in the light of divine truth, then you can feel you are watching the workings of the gift of knowledge. It is not a rational judgement so much as a sort of intuition; and it is a sort of intuition which comes of living with God and so learning, unconsciously, to share His mind.

There are four ways we might think of in which this gift can help us to be single-minded, to see all the manifold in terms of the One, and to avoid being distracted. First of all, it can help us in our judgements about God Himself. We are dependent, at the beginning, for our knowledge of God on the formulas of the faith; and these formulas are created things, necessarily inadequate expressions of the Infinite Reality. It is not these we believe in, but the things they strive to express; but none the less if we misunderstand them, if we read the wrong implications into them, we shall be misled about the Reality. There is always the danger of projecting on to God the purely human qualities, emotions, motivations, standards, with which we are familiar; there is always the danger of sentimentality and self-deception and wishful thinking. The gift of knowledge can help us to keep a sense of God in all our derivative judgements about Him; it can call us back to the central core of truth if our speculations are going awry; it can keep alive and active in us the immediate apprehension of God which guides and determines all our thought about God.

Then, in the second place, the gift of knowledge causes us to judge aright about creatures in themselves, neither despising them (which might mean affronting God their Maker) nor idolizing them (which would mean turning our backs upon Him). They are not just means to our own pleasure or profit; nor are they our final end: and this is easy enough to grasp in theory, but very difficult to live up to in practice. We badly need the constant guidance of the Spirit. How are we in practice to love creatures, and especially men and women, as we ought, and yet not make them a distraction from God? How are we to bring *this* manifold to unity?

We have already seen the answer in the first chapter, where the doctrine of christian detachment was discussed: the love from which, with much grace and much labour, the evil of self-love can little by little be expelled, so that in the end it may become wholly a part of the love of God. Here we need only notice the special danger of the kind of love in which the senses and feelings are involved, because of the special difficulty of supernaturalizing these and restraining their tendency to lead us into independence and defiance of God. If they are part of a true personal love, and if they are adequately governed and guided by the spirit, they can give to love a great power to influence for good, to lead to God. This is their proper function; and only thus can they be purified and supernaturalized. Consequently, we have to avoid the danger of sentimentality; which means that emotion is isolated and made an end in itself, so that there is no sharing in thought and will: emotion, therefore, ceases to be functional, it ceases to play its part in helping the shared life of thought and will to come nearer to God; the relationship is sterile, and instead of becoming gradually a part of the love of God it will, in fact, become inevitably more and more sickly till it dies away altogether.

Still more we have to avoid the danger of sensuality; which means that sense-pleasure is isolated and made an end in itself, so that not only is indulgence sought apart from God, but that in the relationship itself there is no sharing of thought or will or even feeling; there is not only no growth in the unity of mind and heart which leads to God, there is no unity at all, but only isolated individual indulgence: it is not only not love of God, it is love of nothing but oneself.

But where these dangers are being fought against and the emotions and senses are being trained to fulfil their proper

function, then the love which includes them, so far from
being a distraction from God, can be a powerful incentive
to know and love Him better; and it is all the more powerful precisely because of its wholeness—you are engaged,
not just with one element of your nature, but with your
whole personality.

It remains only too true that all this is difficult to achieve
consistently in practice; you need the help of the Spirit, because not only the senses and emotions but the self as a
whole as well will want, at times, to be autonomous, to forget about poverty of spirit and meekness and discomfort.
And you may well need the help of the Spirit, too, to save
you from making these immediate preoccupations exclusive
of the world outside. You will ensure that they are finally
right and Godward-turning if you ensure that they lead you
not to love others less and be less ready to let them invade
your life but to love them more. And you will be doing the
best thing you can to ensure that in all your love you love
not only well but wisely if you remember the gift of knowledge which is given to the docile soul, so that, living always
in the presence of God, you learn to listen always to His
voice.

The third thing with which the gift can help us is the
whole matter of the *technique* of our journey to God. We
act as we ought when our actions are really an expression
of the realities in which we believe; and in general we need
the help of the gift in deciding whether that correspondence
is present in our actions or not. But the essential is to learn
more and more to live all our lives, all our moments, in
God's presence, to keep always close to God; and here we
come inevitably upon the question of a technique. You will
find, in many modern or relatively modern text-books of
the ascetic or mystical life, a detail programme, a more or
less elaborate mechanism, the purpose of which is to train
the mind and will to this fidelity to the presence, but which
may well repel some seekers precisely because of its studied
elaboration, its air of scientific and self-conscious technique.

Is this the freedom of the sons of God, they may say; and can love grow in this chilly atmosphere of formalism and constraint? The answer, for them, may well be, no. We should remember that this sort of method is, in the main, a product of a particular period to which it was suited; there are undoubtedly some to whom it is still not only useful but necessary—unless they have these props, unless they have a clearly-defined structure, they feel at a loss—but there are others for whom it would be disastrous in this as in any other matter, because it would stifle them, because the necessity of adhering to these set plans would be simply a worry and a distraction, and so would defeat its own purpose. For these there are the simpler ways of the older tradition, and they need look no farther. It would be terrible to try to force oneself to obey an unsuitable technique, evolved in a particular period, under the impression that it was the one and only path to perfection : there are many mansions. . . . The essential is to learn to live in God's presence, to make love the background of all thought and desire and action; we need the help of the gift to show us how best we, with our particular temperament and equipment, are to do it.

The same is true of our private prayer; and this is the fourth way in which we need the gift. People sometimes suppose that mental prayer means in practice making use of the elaborate meditations provided in some modern books, with their sections and sub-sections, their rigid framework within which the mind and imagination and will have their carefully allotted and carefully circumscribed part to play. You must not think that this is the only way. They are again the product of a particular period in the Church's history : they will be useful to some, no doubt, but a positive hindrance to others. The older way consisted in the use of a book to turn the mind and heart to God and to make prayer easy : and the use of the book accordingly ceased when, and for as long as, its purpose was fulfilled. Many people will find that without a book, or without some very simple framework to which they can return when their attention has wandered, they will be lost, and apt to find that their time of prayer has been one long distraction; others may quite soon come to the stage at which they no longer need a book at all because it would, in fact, keep them from their union of heart and mind with God. The gift of knowledge should help us, neither to throw over from laziness a habit of formal meditation which is useful to us, nor to cling to it, through lack of courage, when it is really a hindrance.

And what ought we to meditate on? Here again people are sometimes tyrannized over by convention. There is no need to suppose that we must have some vast and grandiose subject for our thoughts: speculative theology has to be turned into prayer, but there is no reason why prayer should be turned into speculative theology. Be simple. Anything that will make *real* to you the life and personality of our Lord, real in the sense of direct awareness instead of knowledge by hearsay or reading; anything that will bring home to you the indwelling of God in the soul and His presence in all His creatures; anything that will help you to see morality in terms of religion: all these things and many others can be the stuff out of which you make your prayer, and the more simply you handle them the better. You should not be afraid of meditating on the most ordinary things, if you can learn to see in these ordinary things not only the purposes but also the presence of God. Learn, for example, to see the symbolism in things,* and not only your immediate prayer but your whole life will be immeasurably enriched.

In all these thoughts about the gift of knowledge we are close to the third beatitude. For they that mourn are they that in their attitude to creatures have achieved identity of will with God, and so have learnt to use creatures not as a distraction from Him but as a way to Him and as a part of their love of Him. It is the same whether you think of your attitude to men and women and all creatures in themselves

* See later, pp. 148 sq.

or whether you think of the use of created methods of coming to God : you need the gift of knowledge precisely to enable you to be of the company of those that mourn, substituting the generous love of creatures for comfort-seeking, or refusing to let a preoccupation with methods be an obstacle between you and the End. For in all these things alike, that is in the last resort what the gift can do : it can give an abiding sense of the abiding Presence in all things, so that at all moments and in all circumstances you start from the conviction : " I *know* that my Redeemer liveth "; and on that knowledge you act and live.

B. THE SACRAMENT OF PENANCE

And Jesus alone remained, and the woman standing in the midst. Then Jesus lifting up himself said to her : Woman, where are they that accused thee ? Hath no man condemned thee ? Who said : No man, Lord. And Jesus said : Neither will I condemn thee. Go, and now sin no more.

JOHN VIII. 10.

We have been considering the fundamental christian para-dox : You must love *nothing* but God, or you insult your Maker; you must love *all* things, or you insult their Maker; and perhaps now the fact that it is only an apparent para-dox is becoming clear. We might say that the key to the whole problem is the omnipresence of God. " He sees God aright who sees Him in all things "; and he sees things aright who sees God's presence within them. The burden of what the men of prayer have to tell us in this connection is just this : that if you fail to see God in things you fail to see the things themselves; and in consequence, if you love them, you are not really loving the things themselves but a part of them. And when you isolate this partial vision, and love it, you tend to make your love a form of self-love —you tend to love things for what they can give you, you, and always you—and so indeed you set yourself up against

God, and so indeed creatures are for you a stumbling-block. But if, on the other hand, you realize that God is " all in all," that He is what is inmost in things as well as what is infinitely apart from them, and that they are meant precisely to bring you to know Him—the visible things, as St. Paul tells us, meant precisely to teach us to see the invisible —and if, therefore, you learn to love things not partially but wholly, then indeed you love all things, and love them the more passionately for loving them wholly, but at the same time you love nothing but God, there is no rivalry, there is only the all-inclusive universality of the divine love itself.

This is the ideal; and for most of us it remains a far-away, a seemingly unattainable ideal. It is so easy to forget the Presence, to isolate things from their own wholeness, and so either to idolize them or to batten on them. That is why, when we think over our attitude to created things, we have need of sorrow and repentance : not because we have loved excessively, but because we have not loved sufficiently, we have been selfish, and so have not loved aright. And so it is natural for us to go on to think of the healing sacrament which can redeem the past and give us hope and renewal of strength for the future. All is not lost because hitherto we have failed; and if we want to see the mercy of God in the fullness of its patience we can see it here, and be humbled and glad. It is never too late to call upon the gentle forgivingness of God : there is more joy in heaven over one sinner doing penance than over ninety-nine just who need not penance. It is never too late; but the mercy goes farther even than that : we can never turn again too often. We are to be forgiven, not seven times, but till seventy times seven —as often as we repent.

The sacrament of penance is, first of all, a tribunal for the administering of justice and judgement. This aspect of it is essential : it means that we must approach it with the humility of confessed criminals, and that we regard punishment as our due; it means that we have to be careful to confess explicitly the exact nature and number of our grave sins—and this we should do briefly and clearly, and without making excuses or wrapping things up in many words; it means, too, that it is right to mention venial sins, at least in general; and all this discipline of self-examination and consciousness of the demands of justice is part of the purpose of the sacrament. But we see it in its fullness when we remember, having all this in mind, that it is Christ our Lord who is the Judge, and when we remember His words to the poor woman whom the Jews were about to stone for her sin,* remember that He is never shocked or incredulous of the depths to which we can sink, and never harsh except to those who are convinced of their own sinlessness; and then we shall not be tempted to let fineness of conscience (in which we grow with the growth of prayer and love) degenerate into meticulousness and anxious fear and scrupulosity. How terrible it is when people allow their confession to be a cause of endless worry to them, when its whole purpose is to bring them back to God and His peace, to renew their courage and strength, and to set them again to live the live of love and joy.

This is indeed the first thing we need to understand about the sacrament : it is not a question of simply ridding the soul of ugly marks which sin has made upon it. In the first place that is to misunderstand the nature of sin : if we must think of it in terms of metaphor, let us think rather of the curing of a disease : we are lucky if a cure takes away every vestige of the disease, and leaves behind it no weakness of constitution, no tendency to fall a victim to it again; and similarly we cannot normally expect that the forgiveness of our sins will remove completely the tendency to evil choice which our own sins have made habitual in us. On the other

*Compare the scene in the synagogue at the very beginning of our Lord's public life when He read to them the words of Isaias "The spirit of the Lord is upon me. Wherefore he hath anointed me to preach the gospel to the *poor*: he hath sent me to *heal* the contrite of heart, to preach *deliverance* to the captive and *sight* to the blind, to *set at liberty* them that are *bruised*, to preach the acceptable year of the Lord and the day of reward." And He said to them: "This day is fulfilled this scripture in your ears." (Luke iv. 18, sqq.)

hand, the sacrament has a second and very positive purpose : it is concerned not only to redeem the past but to fortify us for the future : it is concerned to restore us to God and to His Church, and also to increase our unity with Him and His Church; it is not only healing but upbuilding.

We do well to see this second purpose of the sacrament in the light of the secular struggle of good with evil which we have been considering. Here as elsewhere, the life and power of God in us have more than a merely private purpose : they are given primarily to restore *this* man, *this* woman, to oneness with God, but the oneness has its social responsibility, the healing and strengthening are intended not least to empower them to help in the redemptive activity of Christ in healing and restoring the world. " Go, and now sin no more " is not only a negative command and encouragement : it means, too, " Go now, and by being yourself thus filled with the light and the life help others to come to the light and the life, for that is your vocation as a christian reclaimed."

And again we must see in this more than a giving back of life and power in general. It is not just an abrogation of the past in order to be strong and effective in the future : it is a giving of strength and effectiveness *through* the failures of the past. Even sin has its redemptive purpose; even our own personal sins can be turned to good, and are meant to be turned to good in our lives. The shame and the sorrow increasing the sense of sin, the realisation of the endless patience of God increasing humility and wonder; all this is part of that process of going down to the depths that there we may learn to be poor, to be meek, and to mourn, that then we may be comforted and turned into strong and fearless instruments of God's purposes. We may not sin in order to understand—that way the sense of sin would grow weaker and weaker within us instead of stronger—but having sinned we can use our shame in order to understand : it is part of the deepening influence of suffering in general. But we shall not use this thing as we ought, we shall not turn evil to good as we ought, unless we can find peace in the midst of shame, and joy in the midst of sorrow. If our sins cause us to be always worried and anxious, if our problems make us brood, make us introspective and scrupulous, we defeat this part of the purpose of the sacrament. The priest is not only judge but guide and pastor : you must not expect him to do all your thinking and willing for you, but you are right to ask for help and enlightenment when you have problems you cannot solve for yourself; and when you have thus reached a conclusion or been given a ruling you must cease altogether to worry, you must keep yourself, at all costs, from going back again and again over the old ground, worrying over the possible insufficiency of past confessions or past advice or past decisions. There are times when things you thought too lightly of in the past appear to you in something more like their true colours, yes; and then you do well to take them again, at least silently in your heart, to God; but that is a very different thing from the endless circlings of the scrupulous mind. " Go, and now sin no more ": it is final; it is the password to freedom : the only thing that remains is to take up the labour of life as a labour of love and expiation and joy.

But, on the other hand, we must remember always the condition of all forgiveness and restoration : " as we forgive them that trespass against us." The confessional is no place for the self-complacent. It is better to be a sinner and recognize the fact with humility and sorrow than to avoid all spectacular wrong-doing and be complacent about it. Compare our Lord's attitude to the poor woman with His attitude to the Pharisees. We must never allow ourselves to talk or think about " sinners " unless we have two things very clearly in mind : first, that we mean those who, objectively speaking, are terribly estranged from God and forgetful of Him, but that we do not mean to imply that, where subjective guilt is concerned, we think they are necessarily in as bad a plight as ourselves; and secondly, therefore, that it is no false assumption of humility but a statement of hard fact when we say " pray for *us* sinners "—and that it is a good thing to say it when we have these others in mind. With those conditions fulfilled it is, of course, not only a good thing but a duty to pray for those who have had less opportunity perhaps than we, and who perhaps, had they had as much grace, would have made better use of it.

But we might well pause here a moment to think over the easily unnoticed ways in which we can be self-complacent by being superior. St. Augustine remarks on the stealthy way in which pride can creep in without our noticing it, and destroy what would otherwise have been good deeds. To be intolerant of other people's weaknesses, forgetting our own; to give way to the temptation to show people up; to fall into the self-deception of criticizing in other people the faults we suffer from ourselves—sometimes it is possible to find out our own predominant failings by seeing what failings most arouse our indignation in other people—all these are ways of letting ourselves be conquered by self-complacency, and they can, in consequence, be very serious.

And if you are thus self-complacent you will, of course, find it difficult to forgive others their trespasses. But if you are poor in spirit and meek and filled with the sense of sin, and if you have learnt to mourn in this sense also that you are ready to accept as God's gift not only the enjoyable things He sends but the trying ones, and those trials in particular which come from the angularities, the thoughtlessness, the ingratitude, the spite, of other people, and to accept them in the realization that indeed you deserve nothing better, then indeed you find it easy to forgive, or rather, you scarcely think in terms of forgiving, for you do not think in terms of injuries. And in and by this mourning, too, you will be comforted; for through it you will learn to see more and more clearly and deeply the omnipresence of God, and to achieve a deeper identity of your will with His.

This is a context in which we shall be well advised to keep our eyes open for the petty sins which, precisely because they are so petty, can be dangerous and grave. The sense of sin teaches us that we are each responsible for all because we are a family; it teaches us to ask ourselves how far the failure of the family is due to our own failure; and it reminds us that family squabbles tend to be petty, and that just because they are petty they can be a poison in the family life. The sacrament of penance should make us humble and gay and large-hearted : humble because of the sense of sin, gay because of the renewal of life and freedom, large-hearted because pettiness keeps us isolated from God and self-centred, but the life and the freedom are given us that we may serve God and His family and live in God's love of His family. But we have to be humble and gay and large-hearted precisely *in* our mourning; if we obey the Spirit it is these things we shall find *in* the discipline of the confessional and the sorrow that attends it : it is because, through the power of the sacrament and the gift of the Spirit, we can learn to choose discomfort that we learn these family virtues; and so the family ties bind us more strongly and our love grows and the negative side of penance turns quickly into the positive, and we learn gradually the key to the christian paradox, we learn to love not just the utility or the pleasantness of some things for us but the goodness and beauty of all things in themselves.

It is this idea of the growth of true love as opposed to false or partial love that gives us the clue to the christian doctrine of mortification. To say " Happy are they that mourn " is to say " Happy are they who mortify themselves and take up their cross daily "; but we go astray and forget the beatitude unless we remember that mortification must be based on a real love and awareness of things within the framework of the love of God and His will, and that detachment in general is not insensitivity but love—real love, the love that is defined and measured by Love.

We must be ready to choose discomfort when Love demands it. And of course Love does demand it, first of all because the self-seeking which is so deeply rooted in us is an offence against love.

The first use to which we must put suffering in general and mortification in particular is known as asceticism: training ourselves to be obedient to God by denying ourselves, more than is strictly necessary, the indulgence of our own desires, so that flesh may become less rebellious to spirit and the whole being may, therefore, be free for its service of God.

Secondly, suffering helps us to expiate: we right the balance of justice which our sins have upset, by voluntarily suffering something for the love of God; and indeed this function of suffering need not be confined to satisfying for our own sins merely but may have its share in helping to expiate for the sins of the world. Nor may we allow ourselves to think that, as is sometimes said, this whole idea of expiation by suffering is a practical assertion that pain is something good in itself, something in which God delights for its own sake : there is a deep-rooted instinct in us which makes us feel that those who, by cruelty, have made others suffer should be made to suffer themselves, and it is an instinct which is supported by theology. To be cruel is to increase the evil in the world, to increase the total of violent self-assertion; and it must be put right by a corresponding act in the opposite direction, an act in which the proud self is humbled and made to accept what before it rejected, the existence of an absolute standard—of justice and goodness and love—to which man must conform. So it was that the total self-assertion of the world in defiance of God was expiated by the total self-dedication, the total obedience, of Christ; and it is in this act of expiation that those who suffer now may share—and, if they are living in the love of God, will want to share.

For, thirdly, it is part of love to want to share in the sufferings of those we love (just as the fact of sharing in others' sufferings can cause us to love them, or to love them more). If we can grow sufficiently in the love of Christ we shall begin to want to share in His sufferings simply because they are His sufferings, and incidentally, through this loving and redemptive pain for the world we ourselves shall grow in our love for that world in and for Him.

St. James tells us that trials should be a joy to us because they are the material of patience, which is the "perfect work." Your asceticism should make you trebly patient. It should make you patient with others: with their oddities and foibles, with their slowness, with their weaknesses, with the injuries they do you. It should make you patient with yourself; not worrying about your lack of progress, though sorrowing over it; doing the best you can with the ordinary humble things God gives you to do, and leaving the rest to Him. And it should make you humbly patient, therefore, towards the Providence of God in every detail: learning to accept in peace and calm whatever things come to you, precisely because they come as part of that inclusive Providence —learning, therefore, more and more to care and not to care.

So the effect of mortification, of the sacrament of penance, of the gift of knowledge, will be not to crush the personality but to free it, and to fill it with strength and peace and joy, and so to enable it to seek God more whole-heartedly, to begin to live in His love. At the same time it will be, not to crush your love of creatures, but, on the contrary, to make it more real and deep. It will be, finally, not to withdraw you from God's family but to make you love and serve it better and better for His sake and in His sight; till at the end you can say of the whole world the words of the psalmist: "I have loved, O Lord, the beauty of thy house, and the place where thy glory dwelleth."

CHAPTER VI

HUNGER AND THIRST
AFTER JUSTICE

Blessed are they that hunger and thirst after justice, for they shall have their fill.
MATT. V. 6.

SOME have held that happiness consists in selfishly following the bent of the passion for wealth or pleasure or power: they are wrong, because these instincts thus isolated and so turned to evil are on the contrary an obstacle to happiness. Others have thought that happiness consists in the " active life " as such, in doing rather than being; and again they are wrong, for activity is either a *means* to happiness, or else is itself beatific only as an *overflow* of a state of being. Happiness is not, essentially, something we have but something we are, though we become what we are by doing— and by the way we suffer when suffering is given us, which way is itself a form of doing. But the active life is a social life; and so this beatitude and the next tell us how we should act towards the rest of the family, first as far as justice is concerned, and secondly in regard to the qualities of soul that go beyond the bare demands of justice: generosity and mercy.

Being is more important than doing. It is wrong to think that in order to do great things for the human family you must be endlessly occupied with external activity, with *les œuvres,* that you must be able to point to the arresting visible changes in the face of things, the institutions, the buildings, the movements, that owe their origins to you. The saints often have these things to their credit; but they achieve them almost, as it were, in spite of themselves, certainly rather as an inevitable result and expression of what they *are* than as a studied programme.

There are always some indeed in the world who think themselves great because their brief appearance on the stage is accompanied with much sound and fury : they have much external power, and use it to change, for a time, the face of the earth; but in reality it is they who are as the grass that withers : they go, and the upheavals they caused are at length forgotten, or figure as a tale in the textbooks of history. The power that lives on is the real power, the inner power : the power to move mountains, to tame the animals and bring them back, as St. Francis did, to the human family, the power to charm men to holiness not by what is said merely but by the voice that says it, the personality it expresses. You find a hint or likeness of this power in all the really great : in the men of genius, perhaps, in the great lovers of humanity, in those who are filled with the love of a purpose greater than themselves; but you find it in its fullness in the saints, whose power is more than human since it is the life of the Spirit within them. You find it, above all, in the life of Him from whom the saints' power comes : "and Jesus returned in the *power* of the Spirit into Galilee "; " and they wondered at the *grace* that proceeded from his mouth "; " and they were astonished at his doctrine, for his speech was with *power* "; " and they talked among themselves, saying : What word is this, for with authority and *power* He commandeth the unclean spirits, and they go out?"—as we read in one single chapter of the Gospel.* So it was, too, that when the woman sought to be cured of the issue of blood He said " Who hath touched my garments?" for He knew that power had gone out from Him. And it is not only a power to heal the body or to give physical strength that goes forth : you look Him in the eyes or hear His voice and you are never the same man again, your whole former life is a land to which you can never

*Luke iv.

return. A great Dominican, himself a man in whom there was something of this inner power, once finely said: "When our Lord calls a man a sinner he isn't one—he used to be."

This is the power that lives on long after the one who has it has passed from the earth; for the original influence is handed on to others and to others again, and from generation to generation down the ages of the world; and perhaps those who long after receive of it do not know to whom originally it was due, but one day they will know, and will thank and bless him. This is the power that is real greatness. But the men who have lusted after power and have grasped at it, and made a makeshift with mere externals, and then with these means at their disposal have tortured the world: what achievement will live after them? Perhaps only this, which would never occur to them: that they have been the ignorant, unconscious instruments of a purpose far beyond their understanding, because through the suffering their lust for power has inflicted, the poor and humble and unfortunate have learnt true greatness of heart.

It is not the magnitude, or otherwise, of the work we have to do that should concern us, but the magnitude of the love with which we do it. It is a terrible mistake to suppose that if we simply carry out the commandments externally we have nothing to worry about. That can be no more than lip-service; it can be simply self-culture, the service of the self; and it can be a form of self-complacency and the kind of practical pelagianism which thinks it can get on very well without worrying too much about its radical sinfulness and need of God. Of course we have to try to keep the commandments; but the essential is to try to keep them in such a way that we learn to see more and more clearly our true Centre, to keep our eyes more and more on God and less and less on ourselves, to say "I live, now not I, but Christ liveth in me." There are, in fact, two opposite heresies here which we have to avoid: the one says, If I do right it doesn't matter what I am; the other says, If I am right it doesn't matter what I do. We have to try to live in God, to be right; but we learn to be right only through slowly and painfully trying to do right; and on the other hand if we were really living in God then inevitably we should, as a matter of fact, do right, for we should hunger and thirst after righteousness.

We should hunger and thirst for the realization of God's goodness in the world : with all our hearts we should want that goodness to be expressed and apparent in everything that is in the world, and in everything that is done in the world. We should hunger and thirst after *social* justice. There can be no ivory tower for the christian. We are a family; and we serve God—we do right—if and only if we serve Him through serving, whether through prayer or through action, the family.

First then, let us think of what this thirst for social justice implies. The virtue of justice causes us to " render to every man his due." That is the bare minimum. Some people think to achieve happiness by being unjust, at least in the sense of seizing what they can for themselves without consideration for the rest of the family. That way lies not happiness but unhappiness, because it must lead to loneliness, to isolation from God and man alike. To be happy you must think in terms of the family, and of the family as capable through God-given power of eventually expressing the goodness of God, the ideal shape of things. Justice is the minimum requirement; but because it is the minimum we are not, therefore, to think it unimportant. Unless there is that there can be nothing further; anything else will be poisoned and turned sour, like the grandiose philanthropy, the flourished cheques, of men grown fat on sweated labour.

But the gift takes us farther than the virtue : it gives us, in St. Thomas's phrase, that " insatiable desire " for justice which you find in the saints : not merely that you do your own duty by your fellow-men, but that you are possessed by the desire to see justice done throughout the world. Here we must return to the thought of our solidarity in sin :

wherever injustice is done in the world, I am involved, I must take a share of the blame; and if I am responsible then I must labour to redress the injustice. But I must labour according to my own particular vocation. It is not for everyone to be directly and actively engaged in the righting of social wrongs; there are other ways of sharing in the work. We can help simply by the power of prayer; we can help simply by *being,* simply by having the inner power of goodness within us. Wherever there is injustice against men and women there is a blind or malevolent lack of reverence for men and women; and if you are the sort of person who is possessed by the spirit of reverence, and therefore the sort of person in whom that spirit is apparent and impressive, then simply by being what you are you recall those who come in contact with you to a sense of this form of goodness : you speak not to their minds only, but, perhaps without their realizing it, to the deep places of their hearts, the places from which the impressions of goodness are less likely to fade.

But help, in one way or another, you must. It is terrible when people think that a social conscience is something added on to the christian conscience, a sort of work of supererogation. Thou shalt love thy neighbour as thyself : it is the *stuff* of the christian life; and without it there is nothing but a sham. You can never say that you fulfil the requirements of the virtue of justice and that that is sufficient : christianity is not justice alone, but love; and it is love that the gift helps you to express. You must have the love that is an insatiable desire for justice. You would have to have it at any time and in any period of the world's history : there is always injustice between men, there is always failure to realize in the world the divine will for the world, and for this you would always be bound to work and pray. But when you live in days which are filled with injustice so appalling as to be unimaginable, like the present; when the whole world is torn with the agony of men and women and children; when beyond and beneath the physical horrors there is the dead weight, the stifling pall, of hatred and cruelty and brute stupidity, and when all this is turned explicitly not only against humanity but against the Godhead, so that you have not only a failure to realize the form of goodness in the world but a furious lust to destroy what little of that form of goodness has in fact been achieved—then indeed you need to hunger and thirst after justice with insatiable desire, and you need the gift of the Spirit to save you from despair.

We must not think of justice only in terms of the rights of men : we must think of it primarily in terms of the rights of God, from whom all other rights are derived. Forget these, and your work for humanity will be likely to degenerate into sentimentality and lead only to confusion. It is not enough to have the will to serve humanity; you must have the knowledge : you must know in what justice consists—and we have surely seen enough of man-made definitions of justice. St. Thomas connects this beatitude with the gift of fortitude : the fortitude which expresses an insatiable desire for the respecting of *God's* rights, and which will not be deterred from fighting for those rights, no matter what may come.

But we have to be very careful here. This is not a question of " militant christianity "—of stridency and vulgarity, or of an attempt to preach the Cross at the point of the bayonet. You fight for the cause of love and truth only with the weapons of love and truth. Violence is a sin against love; wanton vulgarity is a sin against truth. The zeal for justice must be meaningless unless we ourselves are just : and to be just is to do just things justly—the manner is important as well as the deed, the means as well as the end. If you want to work for justice you must remember the beatitudes : you must work in poverty of spirit and meekness of heart. This fortitude of the saints is not a melodramatic irruption into the lives and affairs of other men and women against their will : almost you could say the keynote of it was a quality of quietness. The quiet refusal to betray their own integrity of mind for the sake of accommodation with their environment; the quiet refusal to swim with the current in matters of personal behaviour; the quiet refusal to let fear keep them dumb when unambiguous issues do arise, and a declaration is expected of them at least implicitly; a quiet and humble determination to help the other members of the family when it is possible to give help with courtesy: these are the ways in which fortitude is required of us, not with loud-voiced propaganda and advertisement, and the blare of trumpets.

Yet we must not think of this work of fighting for the rights of God in the world as a question merely of opposing what is evil: it is a positive thing, it is a question of working, with insatiable desire, to build up the life of the Church: to build up the vitality of its thought and its love, the integrity and beauty of its worship, the universality of its love in practice. For all these things depend on us. The qualities are there, the power is there, for the Church is the Christ-life on earth. But in another sense the Church is the community of the faithful, the communion of saints but also the communion of sinners: it depends on us whether the love and the power will be fully shown forth to the world. In this sense the vitality of the Church and of its thought and prayer depends on the vitality of our love and thought and prayer; its worship is diminished and degraded if we play our part ill; its love is stifled if we refuse to be filled with it and to allow it to shine forth from us to the world.

We may or may not be called upon, like the martyrs, to die for the Church: we are quite certainly called upon to live for the Church, and that requires fortitude enough, and zeal for justice. You are never to be led by self-love into sinning against justice to men, or into deceiving yourself about what justice, in fact, demands; you are never to let the love of comfort or esteem lead you into frightened silence when you should speak; you are to be as tenacious of God's rights as you are care-free about your own; you are to serve the Church—the life and thought and worship and love of the Church—with insatiable desire for the beauty of God's house; and you are to do all this no matter what inconvenience or suffering or sorrow it may bring: that is what the hunger and thirst after justice implies; and that is the sort of active life, the God-centred life, which will lead to heaven.

This beatitude, then, is the corollary of meekness, and the elucidation of what is meant by mourning. You must try to be care-free about your own well-being, about your own dignity and the esteem of men, so as to be able to turn your mind to the needs of the world and the rights of God. You cannot be zealous unless you are first of all meek. But equally you cannot be zealous unless you have learnt to be among those that mourn: unless the idea of discomfort and suffering for the sake of love has lost its terrors for you and is something you welcome gladly—or at least unless you are ready to face the terrors, and even then the terror that is met with fortitude and endured with love does not quench the soul's joy.

They shall have their fill: and it is more, St. Thomas says, to be comforted in the kingdom than merely to have and possess it, but it is more, again, to have your fill, to have the fullness of comfort which leaves no sorrow unassuaged. There is a sense, indeed, in which this fullness of comfort can only come after: if you hunger and thirst after justice, and suffer for it, your labours and your suffering have their redemptive purpose and effect; you may in this life be despised and rejected as was a greater than you, but you will have helped and healed many directly, and indirectly more perhaps than you can ever count, and the time will come when this your particular family will gather about you and thank you and bless you and lead you to God to beg Him to thank you too, and then indeed your joy will be filled. But even in the midst of the sorrows you will have your fullness of comfort in another sense if you thus suffer gladly for the love of God and in the power of the spirit: first, because

God does not wait until *we* have realized what we have done before thanking us for our service of Him; and secondly because you will work not with the thought of reward but with the joy in giving which is the essence of love. Everything that you do and give with insatiable zeal, everything that with fortitude you suffer or withstand, will be a gift of love, and to give gifts so is not to look for a reward but to have it.

Still, this ability to hunger and thirst after justice depends so much upon humility, and therefore upon the sense of sin, that we may perhaps be wise to return finally to the thought of the incomprehensible courtesy and gentleness of God, who will thank those who bring Him these gifts even though they are able to bring them only because He has given them first. You give Him fidelity, but it is His gift to you; you give Him courage and endurance, but they come from him; you give Him the zeal which is love, but it is only a shared likeness of the eternal Love. When we think long and deeply of these humbling facts, then we can hope to begin to be strong without being hard, to be brave without being arrogant, to hunger and thirst after justice and not after our own glory. And then we may think of the immense fertility of this God-given inner power, the power that heals and comforts and restores : first spreading its roots wider and wider in the soil of the present; and thereafter making life a different, a new thing, perhaps, for unnumbered multitudes from generation to generation down through the ages of the world—we can think of it thus as the seed in our Lord's own simile, the seed growing secretly, growing with the quietness of true zeal, and so turning, in the end, into the mighty tree in which the birds of the air can come and build their nests—even the world of nature being thus, in degree, restored and healed—a tree of life, flowering into paradise.

Such as I love I rebuke and chastise. Be zealous therefore and do penance.
Behold, I stand at the gate and knock. If any man shall hear my voice and open
to me the door I will come in to him and sup with him, and he with me. To him
that shall overcome I will give to sit with me in my throne. . . . He that hath an
ear let him hear what the Spirit saith to the churches.

APOCALYPSE III. 19-22.

These lines from the *Apocalypse* give us a sort of summary of what we have been thinking of so far. Before the
birth to the new life there must be the death of the evil self,
and the death is necessarily a process of rebuke and chastisement, a doing of penance; and the doing of this penance,
this turning from the false centre to the true, is not to be
accomplished without zeal, without the hunger and thirst
for justice that we have just been considering. (We might
recall, too, the words of an earlier preacher of repentance,
to remind ourselves that this process is not purely a private
affair of our own: St. John Baptist, when they ask him,
" What then shall we do?" tells them " He that hath two
coats let him give to him that hath none; and he that hath
meat, let him do in like manner"; we save ourselves
through serving our family.) But this process is not something that we can do; it is something that can be done in
us, if we will. " I stand at the gate and knock"; " hear
what the Spirit saith to the churches." If we are to have the
life and the power of God it can only be by the gift of God;
it is for us to be docile. But then, if we are zealous in our
docility, if our hunger and thirst after justice are intense
enough to make us wholly obedient to the voice of the
Spirit, and if we have the fortitude to overcome the evil self
in us and to labour for the overcoming of the spirit of evil
in the world which is our family, then we shall be invited
to the table, we shall be given to sit in the throne.

Let us think, first of all, of the opposite of zeal, which we

call lukewarmness, and then turn to study more in detail
the virtue and the gift of fortitude.

You find lukewarmness dealt with in the same third chapter of the *Apocalypse*: "I know thy works, that thou art
neither cold nor hot. I would thou wert cold or hot. But
because thou are lukewarm and neither cold nor hot, I will
begin to vomit thee out of my mouth." You think, at first
sight, that this is unfair; that it must surely be better to be
lukewarm than to be downright cold, better to be indifferent
than to hate. But hatred at least implies an interest; there
is at least a possibility that some chastisement which plunges
the soul down to the depths may open our eyes and then
perhaps our hearts. Perfect indifference is the greater insult;
and the more irremediable state of soul. And it is worth
noting that lukewarmness *is* a state of soul, not a sinful act:
a state of soul like the physical condition we call being run
down, a state in which you may catch anything. It is
caused, first of all, by an inattention to venial sin; the area
of what we regard as negligible increases; we begin to think
of grave sins as being, at least in our case, unimportant
peccadilloes; and where it is question not of refraining
from evil but of doing good, then our conscience becomes
less and less exigent, our duties appear to us less and less
exorbitant: we first develop a skill in arguing ourselves out
of obvious duties, and then, as time goes on, cease to bother
to argue. And meanwhile a hard shell of indifference is
forming around the spirit, and stifling it, until in the end
it may well prove impervious to the influence of God and
man alike, impregnable. He stands at the gate and knocks,
but there is no reply. And that is essentially what lukewarmness means: it is not using, not receiving, the life and
power of God; it is in the latter stages a positive resistance
to the offered power, a positive refusal to listen to the voice
of the Spirit. We have no further interest in the life and
the power and the voice: we are bored. So at the end we
find we are in hell—and it is this that makes the eternity
of hell, and the fact of hell at all, an obvious inevitability,

given free will: we have turned ourselves into people of this sort, and people of this sort are precisely people who *cannot* turn again because they have made it impossible, and being unable to turn again they *cannot* live with God, they are eternally, irredeemably, enclosed in their shell of boredom.

Sometimes God, in His mercy, recalls us, just in time. We can never ask forgiveness too late, we can never ask forgiveness too often. But if we are given the mercy, and turn again, it must be as a child that we turn, it must be in poverty and meekness and the humility and shame of self-knowledge. Otherwise our fortitude will be a sham, a passing parade, and we shall sink back again. "Go, and now sin no more" means "Go, and now in *my* power, *my* strength, *my* courage, sin no more."

The virtue of fortitude gives us the strength of soul to do what we ought to do in spite of grave perils or obstacles, mastering fear on the one hand, controlling rashness on the other, for both of these can injure the work to be done. St. Thomas treats of four minor virtues which lead us to act in the same sort of way in regard to less serious obstacles which may confront us: the virtues of great-heartedness, magnificence, patience, perseverance.

Great-heartedness leads us to undertake great and arduous works in every kind of virtue without taking fright at their *magnitude*. As a christian virtue it goes, of course, side by side with humility: it is the greatness of heart of the man who says "I can do all things" only "in Him who strengtheneth me." So, because of its strength, it conquers the pusillanimity which is afraid to do great deeds even though they are within one's power, and takes refuge in false modesty; because of its humility it conquers the presumption which tries to do things which are beyond its powers. It conquers the vainglory which loves to be praised either for things not in themselves praiseworthy, or, as St. Thomas shrewdly remarks, by those who are incapable of mature judgement. It conquers the vanity which takes to itself alone the honour and glory of what is done instead of thanking God; it conquers the ambition which seeks self-glorification, and replaces it by the true ambition which wants to use every talent and do great deeds in obedience to God and for love of Him.

Magnificence is the virtue which will not allow great works for God to be impeded by fear of great *expenditure,* and so is a species of this greatness of heart. And though this is primarily a virtue which concerns those who have the disposal of riches, it is to be found also—and how magnificently—in the poor, who will cheerfully spend the savings of many years in providing a feast for a daughter's wedding or the home-coming of a son. This is the greatness of soul which overcomes both senseless extravagance on the one hand and niggardliness on the other; it is an expression of that spirit of poverty and detachment which we were thinking of before: it is the expression of humility. We are only God's stewards; He gives us things, but so that we may serve the family; and because we must serve the family we may not be wasteful, but we may not be miserly either. Sometimes there are magnificent gifts we can give directly to God, like Mary the sinner with her box of precious spikenard; but always there is the family, always there are the poor, and when we give magnificently to them we give to God.

Patience is the strength to endure present *evils inflicted* by others without being unduly disturbed and abandoning the work in hand: the nagging criticisms, the lack of sympathy and help, the incomprehension, the derision, which can make it so hard to go on. And with it goes what St. Paul calls longanimity: the ability not to be discouraged because the good aimed at is so far off, the road so long.

And perseverance, in its turn, has a similar function: to enable us to go on with the task given us in spite of the *fatigue* and boredom that attend a job that must be taken up again day after day and week after week until it is done.

It is at this point that we come upon the necessity of the *gift* of fortitude. For the virtue, says St. Thomas, gives a

man courage and strength to *sustain* all dangers and difficulties; but the gift goes farther than that; it instils in the
soul a *confidence* that all dangers and difficulties will be
overcome. This, indeed, is something beyond the power of
human nature to perform, for many enterprises are inter-
rupted before their completion by the hand of death; but it
is not beyond the power of the Spirit, who brings men to
eternal life, the completion of all work and the deliverance
from all dangers. So it is the gift of fortitude that you see
in the joy and gaiety of the martyrs, who have *confidence*
that their torments will not cause them to falter, and rob
them of eternal life, but, on the contrary, will take them,
through the power of the Spirit, straight to the arms of
God. And we can see the same sort of confidence and quiet
joy in all the works of the saints: what they build, they
build steadfastly and in tranquillity, and neither apparent
failures during their lives nor the advent of death can dismay them or cause them to lose their confidence in the final
outcome; for all their building is in the hand of God, and
in Him they trust, with all the child's unquestioning trust
that what the father has begun he will see to its conclusion.
So, to hear what the Spirit says, to accept His guidance, is
to work with all one's strength in the present, but to leave
the future in quiet and humble confidence to Him. It is to
be zealous, to have the strength of will of the man; but it is
also to be filled, through the power of the Spirit, with the
freshness and spontaneity, the zest and the enthusiasm, of
the child.

There is a tendency in any age like our own, a *fin du
siècle* period when the world has grown stale, for people to
be ready to argue and discuss and perhaps accept a conclusion to the discussion, abstractly, but never to let this conclusion affect the conduct of real life. Perhaps it is the vice
especially of the " intellectual." Fortitude can give us precisely the motive force that is lacking: it rejuvenates—we
have the water of re-birth—and in its power we can have
the zest and vigour and singlemindedness of the young.

"Be zealous." But we have to remember that this is not necessarily, and certainly not primarily, a question of doing more and more things; it is a question of loving more and more deeply and intensely, and therefore of doing the things we do with more and more fervour. An increase in the quantity and extent of our work will no doubt follow, for if we are filled with love we shall be impelled to give always more and more; but that is the logical order. "The zeal of thy house hath eaten me up"—when that is true of us we shall not be lukewarm in our outward works, and neither shall we run the risk of their being hollow and useless and perhaps harmful. And let us, finally, give full value to the word "house": it is first of all the worship of God that is in question; but the world is the Lord's and the fullness thereof, that too is His house, that too we have to serve with zeal and with fortitude if we want it to be really Him that we serve, for inasmuch as we do it at His call to the least of these little ones, and only so, we do it unto Him.

This zealous care for the house of God and our family suggests some thoughts about the prayer of petition. We need to pray the prayer of awe; we need to pray the prayer of reverent filial piety and love; but we need also the *fiducia mentis,* the boundless trust, which the gift of fortitude gives us—the almost arrogant prayer of petition of the saints. There is nothing that love cannot ask for, if it is part of love to ask for it. The faith that moves mountains is expressed in the prayer that moves mountains. "Ask the Father anything in my name . . ." It is part of the humility which says "I can do all things" to be able to pray for all things. And indeed you have in this boundlessly trusting prayer of the saints the whole essence of christian fortitude : the highest exercise of strength and maturity and self-possession, and the highest degree of leaning on the power of God, meet in the prayer which is at once a total dependence on the divine will and at the same time a prelude to heroic initiative and heroic labour.

What are we to pray for? We are *bound* to ask for all we

need, and for all the needs of those dependent on us, not in detail, of course, but at least in general terms : Give us our daily bread. We are *right* to ask for what we want, but always with the condition, not my will but Thine be done; always, too, with the condition, implicit at least, if it is for the good of the family. It is this conditional quality of all prayer of petition that answers the difficulties of those who feel that it must be a pointless and insulting attempt to alter the almighty providence of God. Since everything is already determined what is the use of this prayer, what is the use of trying to alter the divine decree? The answer is that this prayer does not attempt to alter the divine decree : we pray not against the framework of providence but within the framework of providence. We pray because prayer is one of the forces, the energies, which govern events in the world—as many other non-material things, modes of thought and will and desire, govern events in the world. We pray because in the design of providence this prayer may be fore-ordained to contribute to the bringing about in the world of this event rather than that; and so we pray always with the *fiat voluntas tua,* not my will but Thine; and if the immediate object of the prayer is not to be granted us, still the prayer can never be pointless, can never be wholly unfulfilled, because every prayer which is thus conditional is a prayer for the good of God's family, and in that sense will be heard.

But to pray conditionally is not to pray half-heartedly. We must have the gift of fortitude to go on praying for what we need and for what the family needs when the prayer is not immediately heard—for this too, this perseverance in prayer, may be part of the providence. And if in fact we use to the full this gift of fortitude, if in fact we love God enough and the family enough, then we shall do more than ask : we shall almost demand, and our demands will be heard : for one of the great joys of love is to be able to give when asked, and God is not niggardly in love. It is this certainty of God's will to listen, this *fiducia* of fortitude, that you find in the saints; it is this that you find so fully expressed in the words of the Mother of God at Cana, when she will not even turn her wish into the form of a request, but leaves it as a simple statement, " They have no wine." It is this that takes us beyond the prayer of awe and the prayer of piety, nearer to the prayer which is proper to the children of God, the simple, loving, trustful expression of need and desire.

If any man shall hear my voice and open to me . . . We need this prayer of petition not least *in order that* we may have fortitude in our lives; we shall not hear the voice unless our ears are accustomed to the air through which it breathes : unless we have learnt to listen by learning to pray. The two things, prayer and fortitude, are inter-active therefore : we need fortitude to persevere in prayer in spite of every obstacle of laziness and distraction and aridity and apparent ineffectiveness; we need prayer in order to give us fortitude by giving us the constant sense of the presence of God and His providence. And then, if we learn to acquire this fortitude in prayer and in action alike, if we learn to hear the voice and open the door, to be zealous and turn again and do penance and overcome, then He will see to it that we have, deep within us, the joyous sense that the work will be brought to its proper conclusion for He Himself will be with us and guide and sustain our hands. He will come in to us and sup with us, and we with Him, and we shall have our fill.

He that eateth my flesh and drinketh my blood abideth in me, and I in him.
JOHN VI. 57.

He will come in to us and sup with us, and we with
Him: but it is not only a future beatitude that is offered
to us but a present reality which we can have if we will day
by day. And if we are thinking of our need of fortitude and
of the courage to go on day by day with the work given us,
then it is natural that we should think also of this sacrament
of the daily bread, the sacrament which is intended precisely
to give us the daily renewal of strength for the daily task,
and to fill us with the energy, the life and power, which
will make us do great things for God. " He that eateth
my flesh and drinketh my blood hath everlasting *life* ":
the tense is the present, you have the life here and now, and
so you are filled with power. *Et ambulavit in fortitudine
cibi illius*—he walked in the strength, the fortitude, of that
food forty days and forty nights unto the mount of God.*
But again, the power implies a social responsibility: we
are empowered to live a family life; and this greatest of
the sacraments is precisely the sacrament of *unity*. The
christian's journey is not meant to be a lonely one. But to
achieve a family life you must avoid two opposite dangers:
you must avoid individualism, the private search for a private sanctification; you must equally avoid totalitarianism,
the idea of an imposed uniformity which is the destruction
of the individual. The family of God is meant to be a unity,
but a unity of real living men and women, really bringing
something—a unique creative gift—to the common life.
The Lord's supper is the sacrament of unity because its first

*III Kings xix. 8.

purpose is to cause us to live in the life of Christ, to be one with Him; but also because its effect should be to forge anew the unity of men with one another, and thence to restore also something of the unity of all creatures, since it is the whole of creation which it sanctifies.

The Mass is, first of all, a sacrifice. That is the first way in which it fulfils a universal instinct and desire of mankind. Sacrifice is a necessity because it is part of the nature of the creature to express its dependence on its Creator : to fail to say " In comparison with You I am nothing because all I have and am is from You " is to do violence to one's nature, to attempt, as Adam attempted, to cease to be a creature at all. The essence of sacrifice is this inward offering of the self : why then do we use these material things to express an inward offering ? Because we are not spirit but body-spirit : the use of material things is our natural mode of expression. But there is more than that. This sacrifice is the summary and the fulfilment of all the sacrifices of all the races of the world because the thing offered is Him who is All in all : the self is offered, yes; but it is offered as a part of something much greater, as part of the self-offering of the Infinite made flesh, and therefore as part of the self-offering of the whole world included in that infinite act of offering. You go to Mass to offer yourself to God; but you are part of the self-offering of the whole Church in Christ who redeems and sanctifies the whole world; and so you take with you the whole of creation, for " the whole of creation is in travail even till now," waiting to be " delivered from the servitude of corruption, into the liberty of the glory of the children of God."* So with the bread and wine of the sacrifice you offer the earth and the fullness thereof, the things that grow and are meant to minister to man's needs and give him joy; in the song and gesture and movement of the Mass, and in the stones and glass, the carvings and paintings, that house and adorn it you offer all the arts of man; the symbols of the evangelists are there to

*Romans viii. 21.

remind you that the beasts, too, share in the travail of creation, and must share in its restoration. Everything in your own life must be offered in order to be cleansed and transformed by being caught up into this single cosmic act of worship; but everything in the world must be offered, too, and for the same purpose.

The sacrifice of the Mass is one and the same as that of the Cross: you are taking part in Calvary. Christ is not simply an historical figure, now gone from the earth. The Mass *is* the sacrifice of Calvary because Priest and Victim are in each the same: it is one and the same Christ who offers and is offered. Christ is with us in the world today. But moreover, when you take part in the Mass the curtains of time are rolled back and you step into the eternal present because the Mass transcends time: you are taking part in an eternal act of will. The agony, the way of the Cross, the death on the Cross, these are events in the past; but these are the physical and historical expression of an act of will of a Man who is also the God in whom there is no change. The mode changes, the substance remains the same. Your own self-offering and your offering of the world which is your family are raised to infinity because they are included in this single act of self-offering of a Victim who is divine. So in the offering all things are made one: and this is the second way in which the Mass fulfils the universal instinct and desire of mankind.

But the Mass is also a sacrament, the means whereby this redemptive act is made operative day by day in the world. Creation waits for delivery from the servitude of corruption, waits for the liberty of the glory of the children of God: and it is not a forlorn hope but an expectancy precisely because of the Mass, which is the centre of the whole sacramental system, of that economy whereby the life and the power are given to souls and so spread abroad in the earth, because it is through the Mass above all that Christ is with us, the sacrificial Christ. God is everywhere, is All in all. But here you have a new, a redemptive presence: it is the redeeming

Christ who through the Mass is still with the earth to save
and heal and bless it, who through the Mass can walk again
the lanes and fields of England, who through the Mass visits
the slums and tenements, and weeps now over the battle-
fields and the bombed cities as once over Jerusalem. And
the presence of this redeeming love and power, this promise
of liberty and glory to a world in servitude—for the power
is able, if only we will use it, not only to transform into
spiritual splendour the squalors and sufferings begotten of
injustice, but still more to overcome in the end the spirit
of evil which produces the squalors—this is the third way
in which the Mass fulfils the desire of mankind.

We shall not see the Mass aright unless we realize that
sacrament and sacrifice are one : we must not separate the
joy of the supper from the sacrificial death. Let us think,
first of all, of the lesson of the structure of the Mass. There
is the great historical division : the Mass of the Catechumens
first, and then from the offertory onwards the Mass of the
Faithful from which all but the baptized were excluded.
And each of these main parts comprises a twofold movement : there is first the offering to God, and only then the
receiving of the gift from God. You have the confession of
sins, the prayer for mercy in the *Kyrie,* the song of praise
which is the *Gloria,* and then the collects—the *united*
prayers for the needs of all; and then, when this duty of
offering of prayer has been fulfilled, you have the gift from
God : the gift of the truth in epistle and gospel. Similarly
with the main part of the Mass : offerty and consecration
come first, and only then the gift from God, the supper.

The offering to God is an offering of sorrow, praise and
thanks. But it is an offering *per Christum, through* Christ
and *with* Christ; and it is an offering which is made perfect
because through the sacrament it is made not only with
Christ but *in* Christ. *Tu mutaberis in Me* : you shall be
changed into Me. But if in Christ, then in the unity of the
family also whose Head He is. Pray, brethren, the priest
tells us, that my sacrifice and yours may be acceptable. It is

the sacrifice of the whole family, and we are all the offerers; the act of worship is a social act of worship. That is the importance of the present renewal of the Church's liturgy : it is not primarily an aesthetic reform, but a theological. The Mass is not a spectacle at which the faithful are to assist, but an act in which they are to take part. Hence the value, where the integrity of High Mass is impossible, of the dialogue Mass : at least you are taking your share in the action. And you are taking your share, not only with the official priest at the altar, but with your brothers and sisters in the church. In the primitive days there was the immediate connection of the Mass with the Agape, the love-feast of the faithful; nowadays there is the same thing expressed in symbol in the ceremony of the *pax* at High Mass, the kiss of peace. If you bring your gift to the altar and there remember that your brother has anything against you, you must go first and be reconciled. The supper is a family feast.

You shall be changed into Me : it is the whole family which is thus to be changed, and by being changed to become a unity. That reverence which we should feel for all God's creatures and in particular for men and women is here intensified a thousandfold, for we have now to see Christ Himself in one another. If you meet a procession of the blessed Sacrament, if you meet a priest taking the Viaticum to the house of someone who is sick, you recognise the Presence and kneel : and if you meet those who have just come from the altar will you ignore this same Presence within them? For they, too, are the bearers of God into the world. It is a good thing to think of the sins against charity, the sins we are sometimes inclined to regard as of small consequence, in this light : how, when we have supped at this same table and gone out again into the world with Infinity in our hearts, how can we so soon forget, and fall into these petty sins which are so grave a betrayal of love and reverence?

And it is the *sacrificed* Christ that we receive; and so the sacrament is a sacrament of unity in a yet wider sense. We

are to be one body, not in any sectarian and exclusive sense;
we are to be a unity, not *against* the world without; but
precisely in order that, in the strength of this common life,
we may together be bearers of God into the world; and
learning, through poverty, meekness and the rest, to be
transparent of God may help to make possible in it His
redemptive purposes.

This is indeed what the common priesthood of the faithful implies. And this is surely why the ending of the Mass,
after the Communion, is so short compared with the lengthy
preparation. The Communion done, there are the brief
communion and post-communion prayers and then " Go,
the Mass is ended." Why? Because this ending is precisely
a beginning : you are to go and take up the daily task, you
are to go and do your work in the world, you are to go and
make operative in the world the sacrifice you have just
offered and received.* The Mass is the central point in the
day : all the Church's liturgy, the divine Office, centres in
it; all the prayer of the faithful centres in the Office; all
the work is to be turned into prayer, and so into the
Church's prayer, and so into the Mass. And similarly with
the downward movement of blessing from God : it is the
Mass above all which gives the official and unofficial prayer
of the family, and all the work of the family, their value
and their redemptive power : Go, then, and begin your
work in the strength of that food; go and spread about you
in the world the power of love because now you have Love
within you, you are abiding in Him and He in you.

It is part of the integrity of family life, as we shall see, to
be outward-turning, to be not an enclosed and aloof community but a centre of life and light for the world outside.
And what is true of the human home is true of the greater
home which is the Church. " I will draw all things to Me,"
He said; but His will is to make His family, His Church,

* This, of course, does not mean that we should not stay a little after
the Mass, to be close in love and worship to Him who has been given us,
and to thank Him for the mercy thus shown us in spite of our sin, and
the blessing thus given to the day which lies before us.

an invitation in His name. Sometimes we are not an invitation but an obstacle. Many are seeking Him, and without success: they have heard that He is the God of Love and they look for His presence among men and fail to find it—and is it always their fault? When you have a family which is obviously a unity forged by love, and a love so strong that it radiates outwards and colours the world about it, then you say "Love lives there"—but is our religious family like that? This is the failure we should regret most bitterly, and most vigorously determine to remedy: we bear within us the Infinity which can heal the entire world: and instead of acting in that power and blessing the world and bringing it peace and unity and happiness we increase the discords and divisions, we prolong the travail and the pain. So we turn directly against the purpose of the sacrament. He that eateth my flesh and drinketh my blood abideth in Me and I in him: to live in Christ *must* include as its secondary effect to share Christ's love of creation and so to share in His work for the healing of creation.

St. Thomas Aquinas is honoured as the Doctor of the Eucharist. It is very fitting; and not only because he wrote of this sacrament itself supremely well. The Eucharist is the greatest restoring power in the world, and for the world: in it all things are made new. It is then the greatest affirmation of the value of created things, of their goodness, for if anything were wholly evil it could not be restored; and so it is the great affirmation also of the unity of all things in that single act of worship and sacrifice which is the Cross. But it is just this that is the essence of St. Thomas's teaching. When he is writing of marriage he speaks of manicheism, with his usual exactitude, as *pessima haeresis,* the worst of heresies: you cannot say that matter is evil for this, too, comes from God, and, where man is concerned, is an essential part of worship. Nor, for St. Thomas, can there be that opposition between this world and the next, between nature and grace, which you find in some christian thinkers: the divine life works in and

through nature, it is engraced nature which has to serve
and worship God, and labour to remedy as far as may be the
effects of the original turning away. He is the Doctor of
the Eucharist, then, because he is the expounder of this
great affirmation : all things are good in themselves though
evil has damaged and twisted them; all things are renewed
and blessed by the presence of the sacrificed Christ in the
world, by the power of Christ made operative through the
souls and bodies of His faithful who share His life and
His love. But the corollary of this affirmation, the affirmation of the liberty of the glory of the sons of God, is the
giving of thanks; and this is what the word eucharist means,
and in this, too, therefore the title is justified. "To them
that love God all things work together unto good": that
loving sense of the ceaseless providence of God, the sense
that what is is His will and therefore must work unto good,
and that all our efforts are but part of that all-inclusive love
and care so that we, for our part, are free, carefree, if only
we do at each present moment the best we can—all this
conviction, together with the deep happiness it produces, is
in our belief in the Eucharist, and therefore is an essential
part of our worship when we worship, as we must, through
the Eucharist.

"I draw all things to Myself"; and "behold I make all
things new"; that is the summary of the doctrine of the
Eucharist; and to say that we must share in this double
movement is to summarize our part in the doctrine of the
Eucharist. If ever it could be said of us that all our words
were enlightenment and solace and strength, our touch
always a healing touch, our eyes wise and gentle, our whole
life an epiphany of the power of love—then it would mean
that we had been fully faithful at last to the greatest of all
the sacraments, because of us as of Him in whom we live
men would be able to say "we have seen their glory; and
of their fullness we have all received."

CHAPTER VII

THE DIVINE PITY

Blessed are the merciful, for they shall obtain mercy.

MATT. V. 7.

In this fifth beatitude we are given a yet more emphatic repudiation of the policy of the ivory tower. We are all involved in the life of the family, and all responsible for it: we have, as we have seen, a duty towards it in justice; but justice is not enough. And indeed, once you accept the idea that the race of man is God's family and yours, the fact that justice is not enough becomes obvious: who could imagine a happy family life based exclusively on justice? St. Thomas remarks that " some withdraw themselves from works of mercy *lest* they be involved in other people's misery "; most of us would have to plead guilty to doing just this at some time or another—" I simply cannot go and see that poor old woman; it makes me miserable for the rest of the day "—but it is clearly the denial of the whole substance of family life. And our Lord is quite definite: it is not by doing this that we shall find happiness, but by doing exactly the contrary, by being merciful. Why? The first reason is already stated: only by being merciful can you live in the family, and only by living the life of the family can you be fully alive. But there is a second reason. St. Thomas has a further remark which at first sight may seem somewhat arbitrary: this beatitude, he says, is connected with the gift of counsel, which concerns the choice of means to attain the desired end, and which, therefore, particularly concerns " those things which are *most* useful to the end, namely, mercy." And why is mercy thus singled out above all other good qualities? Surely because it is the greatest

possible repudiation of the kingdom of Mammon, at the
farthest possible remove from the selfish struggle for *my*
rights, *my* pleasure, *my* comfort, *my* privacy. Mercy is in
those who have already learnt to think and to will in terms
of the family.

Justice is not enough. You have here a virtue which goes
beyond the demands of justice, the virtue of generosity,
which leads us, says St. Thomas, to give freely to friends
and others who are specially united to us, and with whom,
therefore, we do not think in terms of mere justice. Poverty,
detachment, make us open-handed; meekness and the ability
to choose discomfort make us further forgetful of ourselves;
fortitude gives us the large-heartedness which can be magnificent in its giving; and the love which is the stuff of real
friendship as of family life makes us long to give lavishly,
for in love it is giving which is itself the highest form of
receiving.

But beyond the virtue there is the gift.* We are right to
have a special place in our hearts for our own family and
our own friends; but if we are to live as christians then the
whole world has to be our family, and all men our friends.
The gift goes farther because it considers one thing only:
the *need* of others. In the last chapter we were thinking of
the Lord's supper; and now we are in the context of the
parable of the supper: "Go out into the highways and
hedges and *compel* them to come in, that my table may be
filled." The gift considers only the need of the outcasts,
the publicans and sinners, the waifs and strays, and because
of their need must give them a special love and reverence.
Let us underline this word reverence in our minds: unless
we have this we may have pity indeed, but not the pity
which is the gift of the Spirit. For this pity you learn by

* St. Thomas, as we have just seen, links this beatitude with the gift of
counsel ; elsewhere he connects it with the gift of piety. Here, for the
sake of brevity, I speak simply of the "gift of pity", meaning by that
the impulse of the Spirit through these gifts in teaching, inspiring and
directing the soul in the way of the merciful.

learning to be reverent and docile towards God; it is a gift you *receive*; and when you hold it out in your hands to another you must remember whence it came, you must remember that only in abasement of spirit can you pass on a gift which is divine, you must remember and imitate the pity of Mary the sinner when she anointed the feet of Christ, a pity which was divine precisely because in one and the same action she expressed her own abasement and sorrow, and her pity for the wayworn feet of God.

We are here at the very centre of the way of perfection. If you would be perfect, go, sell all you have and give to the poor : in the literal sense it is the poverty of the vows and the cloister, but its spirit is not to be confined to the cloister, for its spirit is simply the ideal of charity. Be ready to give anything you have when your brother is in need; be ready to sacrifice your possessions, your comfort, your time, all that you have, not only for the sake of those who are dearest to you, but for the sake of any of the outcasts : compel them to come in, compel them with the power of love, that the table may be filled—and what a glory it is to bring the suffering and the needy to God's table.

We are at the centre of the way of perfection because we are exactly at that point where the faith becomes not something acknowledged with the mind but something burning and shining through the heart that all may see; we are at the point where the love of God does, in truth, become that ocular demonstration of the Gospel for which the world is waiting and looking. " See how these christians love one another!"—they have heard it said so often in derision down the ages of history; they miss the innumerable humble lives in which it has been a blazing truth, and see only the scandals of the sects and schisms and wars and hatreds which have stained and rent the seamless robe of Christ; but live this beatitude, learn to make your whole life an expression and fulfilment, a channel, of the divine pity, and they will forget all they have heard, they will forget all they have

learnt from their history books, because they will be able
to look into your heart and see His glory, the glory of the
only begotten of the Father, full of grace and truth.

Why, people ask, are the christians no better than the
non-christians, if all that they claim for their faith is true?
And the answer, in so far as the accusation is a true one,
must be that we are influenced far more deeply than we
know by the individualism we inherit and the selfish
materialism with which we are surrounded. We are busy
with the defence of man's right to property, and so we must
be; but only if we remember that we are advocating no
absolute right, only if we take care that in opposing one
error we do not fall into a worse one. We have a right to
property, yes; but every right implies a corresponding duty,
the right to property implies a duty to the common good—
and the more we have, the greater our responsibility for that
common good. We have a right to property, but only within
the life of charity. We have a right to a house, a home; but
it must be, not a fortress from which all are excluded, but
a home where all can find a welcome.

And as with material possessions of every sort, so with all
that we have and are, the gift enables us to be humbly and
royally lavish, and above all with the gift of pity itself. You
must be lavish, first of all, to those nearest to you, those you
love most; but you must be lavish, too, to those who are
most in need; you must be lavish to your enemies—or rather
to those who think themselves your enemies, for it takes
two to make an enemy. You must have pity for all, and
the greatest pity for those who have greatest need of it.
But humbly, reverently, not conferring a gift but asking to
be given one; otherwise you will have not pity but the terrifying vulgarity of condescension and all the ugliness of
pride. (Think for a moment of whether you are ever
"shocked" in the colloquial sense of the word : if you are
it is a lack of wisdom, for you ought to know more about
human nature, including your own; it is a lack of humility,
for you are presupposing that the thing that shocks you is

something far below your own moral level—and if that is the way you think you will never have the gift of divine pity.)

We have been thinking much of the life of the family. Think a little of this gift of pity in terms of family life : it is easy, then, to apply it to the larger family of the world. Think first of the perhaps unconscious, perhaps hotly repudiated, need of the young for pity from the old, and of how easy it is to forget that need and so to be destructive : you forget or you deride and lacerate the keen sensitiveness, the soaring hopes, the innocence that goes with the lack of hard, and hardening, experience. If you have pity for these things you can strengthen and up-build, where necessary you can heal and restore; without pity you may easily turn growing experience into poison and despair. Think, on the other hand, of the need of the old for pity from the young. Remember the pathos of the divine words to Peter : " But when thou art old another shall gird thee, and shall lead thee whither thou wouldst not." Remember the long pain of dwindling strength and power, the loneliness of those whose friends have left them behind, the sorrow of happier memories, the feeling of becoming a stranger as the younger generations establish their new, strange ways; remember that the slownesses, the disabilities of mind and body, the oddities of behaviour which most arouse the impatience of the young, are themselves a cross and perhaps the result of many earlier crosses. And again if you have pity for these things you can give strength as well as solace, and perhaps you can turn a purgatory into a joy; but if you lack pity you may well bring bitterness into the last days of a human life —and how shall you efface *that* stain?"

Remember the Mass, to which all creation is brought that it may be redeemed and blessed. We must not think of bringing only the lovely things and the noble things and the things of good report : we are to bring the sorrows and uglinesses of the world that they may be cleansed; we are to bring the heart of man that it may be purified and made

gentle, and piteous of human sin and human stupidity as
Christ was piteous. For when you remember the Mass you
remember the Cross : you remember what the eyes of
Christ beheld from the height of the Cross—not only the
immediate unimaginable crime and the malice of those
who watched and jeered, but all the sin in all the hearts of
men then living, and then backward through the ages all
the sin from the beginning, and onward into future ages
to the end of time even though now the Light was in the
world—you remember all the weight of all the evil of all
creation : and then you remember that He prayed for them
because they were ignorant.

Remember the tears of Christ that were shed in pity over
Jerusalem; but do not think that this is something which is
faded into the past; do not think that though God could
weep over Jerusalem He cannot weep now over the sorrows
of earthly cities. The tears were shed at a moment in time,
yes; but God is not in time, and the sorrow and pity of
God are present with us, with every cry and tear drawn
from men's bewildered—or perhaps hardened and blas-
phemous—hearts; the eyes of Christ wept, and now can
weep no more, but the actions of Christ are the actions of
God in whom is no change, no past, no history, but the
single moment of the eternal present; and because of the
Incarnation of the Word there is unchangeably in the heart
of that eternal present the mystery of the pity and sorrow
of God.

But we must understand pity aright, as we must understand comfort aright. The pity of Christ, the pity which is
this gift of the Spirit, is a *redemptive* pity, the pity that
heals and strengthens and up-builds, the pity that said to
the poor woman " Go, and now sin no more." That is why
you are so immeasurably far from the withering pride of
condescension : the quality of this mercy is not strained
(for it has the freedom from all narrowness, all bounds, all
reserves and inhibiting prejudices, of the wind that bloweth
where it listeth); it droppeth as the gentle rain from heaven,

the rain that makes the earth fertile, and renews it and causes it to bring forth again its fruit; it is the healing touch that raises men and restores them to wholeness and gives them the courage to start again.

Perhaps that is what you must have most pity for, as Christ would seem to have done: the sin of the world that comes of stupidity. You must never, of course, for an instant let your pity be degraded into sentimentality, so that you cease to regard sin as important or culpable, or brush away with a gesture the real evils, the pride and malice and cruelty, that tear the world. But there is so much wrongdoing that springs from ignorance; they know not what they do, they are deluded or their judgements are mistaken; sometimes the sins against Christ and His Church can be an attempt to serve Christ and His Church. And then there are all the sins of human frailty: the flesh lusteth against the spirit, and we do those things we would not do; and for these too, in others, you must have pity. The quality of mercy is not strained.

"He that hath the substance of this world and shall see his brother in need and shall shut up his bowels from him: how doth the charity of God abide in him?" Perhaps you have the substance of eternal life, the gift of faith which is yours through no merit of your own; and if you see your brother in need of this, and shut up your bowels from him, how shall the charity of God abide in you? Think, in this connection, once again of the petty sins: the censoriousness, the scandal-mongering, the touchiness and ill-temper, the desire to show people up, to prove your own superiority; think of all the small nagging ways in which the life of the family can be withered and made parched and arid, and compare it with this gentle rain from heaven: then the sense of sin will grow in you, and with it the sense of pity, for the two go together. "Forgive us our trespasses as we forgive them that trespass against us," if you have pity for others you will obtain mercy yourself, but equally if you know in the depths of your soul your own need of mercy you will have pity for your brother, and your pity will be the divine pity because your offering of it will itself be the asking of a favour.   "Behold, I stand at the gate and knock"; omnipotence becomes a mendicant because it is part of the nature of love that it must ask to be allowed to give.

La colère des imbéciles remplit le monde—the world is filled, and racked and torn, by the fury of fools, and the base things are exalted and the lovely things destroyed; but still you must have pity.

And if you are a woman, then remember that this is your special vocation, the vocation of woman; and until you have fulfilled that vocation you will never be made whole. The male mind, the rational mind, has its schemes and ambitions; it tries to order the economy of the world, to marshal events and dictate policies and build up the outward structure of life; and it has great pride, the pride of the creator, in its achievements, and it likes to think that it is self-sufficient, and that it battles with destiny and orders chaos alone and unaided. But reason without intuition, the male without the female mind, is often blind and often stupid; and one day its house of cards falls about it, the long labour and the mighty ambitions are turned to dust, and then there is emptiness. And then it is time for you to fulfil your vocation; to have pity on the rational stupidity of men. The gentle rain has to fall on the withered soil of the soul of the man and renew it; you have to have pity in order to heal and restore and re-create; and then in your pity you yourself are made whole. You will not be made whole until then, until you have let this fumbling arrogance grope its way to your different and deeper wisdom and from the womb of your pity be born again.   "Son, behold thy mother": you have in Mary the Mother of Mercy the figure of what you have to be. It may be particular men—husband, children, friends—who will come to you so; it may be your vocation to share with Mary something of her universal pity, but to renew the soil of the world only indirectly, through your own inner experience and your un-expressed pity. But somehow, in some way, you must share her vocation, you must share the glory of the destiny of which she is the symbol and the supreme expression; for only so can you share as you should in the restoring of the world, and only so will you yourself be made whole.

It is the special vocation of woman; but of course it is not confined to woman. Those specially whose gift it is to have in a marked degree the qualities of mind of both man and woman, to be rational and intuitive : the artists and men of genius; those whose special office requires this two-sided quality of mind : the priest who is representative of *Mother* Church, the doctors and surgeons whose special vocation is to heal; those who have care of the frailness of childhood—all these have a special need of the gift of pity if they, in their turn, are to be made whole, and through their special destinies to serve the world. But the substance of the gift of pity all of us must have, if we are to obtain pity; and all of us will, in fact, have it if we have learnt to be humble and to mourn.

For pity is indeed the corollary of humility and repen-tance : you can no longer, if you have learnt the sense of sin, speak of your brother with arrogance as a sinner. We are each responsible for all. You will not say, when you see some evil done, "There but for the grace of God go I"; you will say "There go I." You will not say "How these are hurting the heart of Christ," but "How I in these am hurting the heart of Christ." For you will know yourself implicated, responsible; and there will be shame and sorrow in your pity because you have not done more to avert the evil, have not perhaps even prayed for these who are the immediate cause of the evil. But you will hardly think in terms of praying for sinners : you will think of praying for others, and especially of praying for your sin in others : these, you will say, have gone astray and perhaps are at war with the Good, but why has not power gone forth from me to help to heal them, as it went forth from Him who has sent me to be a bearer of His power? These are searching for God, and are miserable because they cannot find Him, and have I even prayed that they may find Him?

Let us repeat: we must never for an instant allow pity to degenerate into sentimentality: we must be as hard as iron in our estimate of the gravity and the horror of sin; we must never minimize anything, never excuse anything by explaining it away. Pity essentially depends on clarity of vision: you become most fully merciful when you become clean of heart. But you must be able to see the two things with equal clarity: the nature of sin in itself, the immaturity in evil of the human heart.

There is something more. You will degrade your pity, perhaps you will destroy altogether the power of pity in you, if you pity yourself. If there is one thing more humiliating than to say "How good I am" it is to say "How unfortunate and ill-treated I am." The essential condition of this gift of divine pity for others is to be convinced, not of your need of pity for your sad fate, but of your need of mercy for your sins. If you are the victim of self-pity you may feel sad and sympathetic for others, though it is hardly likely perhaps; but your pity will certainly stop short at the softness of solace: it will be unable to strengthen and upbuild. And that is the whole purpose of the pity which is divine. If, on the other hand, you know your own need of mercy, then your eyes will be turned on God; you will be able to be the instrument of His own gift of pity, and so you will give new heart to others, you will not only console, but strengthen and sustain.

Happy are the merciful, for they shall obtain mercy. To obtain mercy, says St. Thomas, is more even than to have one's fill, because it means that man receives more than he merited or *was even able to desire*. If we have the sense of sin we want God's mercy; and to receive that is much indeed; but we need his mercy more than we want it, for we need it more than we can know. But there is more even than that. The merciful shall obtain more even than they can desire: and how is that? Because pity enlarges the heart, and where there is infinite pity there is an infinite enlargement of the heart, and so an infinite capacity for joy—and what the joy is, no man can tell.

A.   THE PAIN OF THE WORLD AND THE GIFT OF COUNSEL

Amen, amen I say to you, unless the grain of wheat falling into the ground die, itself remaineth alone. But if it die it bringeth forth much fruit. . . . If any man minister to me, let him follow me : and where I am, there also shall my minister be.
JOHN XII. 25, 26.

The gift of counsel is concerned with the choice of means to the desired end. You have to make your whole life a single Godward movement, so that everything that you do and have and are becomes functional, becomes part of that movement. You have, therefore, to see all that happens in the light of the unity of God's providence. For all this you need the gift of counsel; and you need it specially where it is specially hard to see God's love and providence: in the problem of pain.*

There are two extreme positions, both of them unchristian. There is first the quest of invulnerability: the determination to avoid pain at all costs, as being the greatest of all evils. This is un-christian because it refuses to see that pain can often have a positive value: not only as an ascetic training of character, but as a means to a deeper awareness and understanding. On the other hand, there is the glorification of pain as something good in itself, an end rather than a means, so that all attempts to alleviate it—by increased medical skill, for example—are regarded as immoral.

*We have already mentioned the christian doctrine of the threefold value of suffering for the christian himself. Here we are concerned not with this but simply with the attempt to find, for the onlooker, some explanation of the problem of pain.

This attitude is un-christian too, for it forgets, or at least minimizes, the redemptive presence of Christ in the world : there is sin and therefore there is suffering, but the life and the power are with us to overcome the sin and in some degree to alleviate, or to transform, the suffering, as the Church does by prayer and the laying on of hands. Pain is an effect of evil; it can also be a means to good; but if you make it not a means but an end you deny the nature of God, and blaspheme.

The christian position then is neither of these extremes. It accepts pain, directly as the effect of evil in the world, indirectly as a gift from God, since out of evil good may come. It acknowledges the duty of redeeming the world from pain in the end; but it acknowledges the duty of redeeming the world *through* pain, as a means. Pain has its redemptive purpose; but sometimes it is hard to see this, and often it is hard to accept the fact and act accordingly : we need the gift of counsel.

We need the gift of counsel to see clearly ourselves, and still more to be able to help others to see. If you misunderstand and misinterpret the christian attitude you can do great harm : if you turn it into something morbid, if you treat pain as good in itself, you turn the religion of love into a grey cult that kills the joy in life and makes a travesty of the goodness of God. And the misinterpretation leads, in practice, to disaster : the Church has always taught man's need of gaiety and joy, and if you deny this wisdom you destroy the health of the spirit and end in neurosis or in death of soul. Suffering is a means to an end; and therefore there is a reason for it : it is part of the plot of a love-story; and we must see it as such.

Does God rejoice in suffering, yes or no? There has to be a double answer. In itself, no; of course not; good cannot rejoice in evil as such. As a means from which good will come, yes, if by rejoicing you mean a willing of the end which therefore includes the indirect willing of the means, and is accompanied by pity. Only thus indirectly is suffering caused by God : the good His love wills for us may have the effect of hurting us here and now; but the hurt is not what He directly wills, and that it *is* a hurt for us is the result of our sin. In giving man the gift of freedom He gives him the freedom to sin, and from sin the evil of suffering follows; but also by suffering the sin can be expiated and its effects in some measure remedied. The pain of the world is not the final thing, as sin itself is not the final thing : the Word was made flesh, and dwells amongst us; the power to restore the world is in the world; the revelation of the glory is given us if we have eyes to see; and it is compatible with goodness and pity to rejoice in the fact of suffering if the suffering is what causes us to see.

That is exactly what suffering can, in fact, do, and why it is part of the plot of the love-story. Sin, and therefore suffering, are permitted by the eternal providence because after sin is the Cross, and in the Cross the revelation of the depths of love, the mercy and the pity, of God. You need suffering of one sort or another to become adult in love; you need it to understand the depths of love and the depths of pity because you need it in order to *experience* the deepest truths and realities. But does that explain the sufferings of children, and of the animals? Does it explain, not the ready acceptance of necessary suffering, but the desire for suffering which is not inevitable, on the part of the saints? No; there is something more.

The saint *must* share Christ's suffering, as we have seen. It is the nature of love. But also we are a family : we are each responsible for all. Your suffering is meant to be redemptive, but not for yourself merely, but for the world. The pain of Christ is redemptive for all humanity, to bring to all humanity the gifts of understanding and love and sorrow; and you can share by your own pain, and if you love Christ enough you will be impelled to share, in that universality. There are mysteries of substitution which we cannot fathom but which the saints have sensed : their choice of avoidable pain is not an assertion that pain is an end in itself, but, among other things, a living proof that we are a family.

But what of the children and the animals? You must go deeper still. These things are in themselves part of that chain of cause and effect which the primal evil set in motion in the world. But though we are all involved because we are all responsible for evil, and therefore must avert or diminish the pain where we can, that is not all. We are a family even when we remain unconscious of our oneness: wherever pain is, there the deeper realities can be revealed to the world; the child, the animal, in pain can so share in Christ's redemptive pity. But they themselves have nothing from it? They themselves remain simply the innocent victims of the evil of the world, and have no recompense? On the contrary. The providence of God is not made ineffective by the creature's unawareness of it: you can begin to work out your salvation from evil, you can be led by God towards His mercy and your own restoration, even though you are unaware of what is being done in you. " He that is mighty hath done great things in me "—perhaps there is an echo of this receiving of an unlooked-for glory in the effect of uncomprehended suffering: we do not know what glory springs for the child in eternity from its puzzled pain on earth; and may not God also, in His mercy, be fashioning its soul secretly to depths of love and understanding which it would otherwise miss? His power to mould us is not limited to an appeal to the conscious mind.

But the animal has no immortal soul? None the less, there are three things which perhaps we can say. First, we must not be sentimental: we must not pretend to ourselves that animals have the same consciousness, and therefore the same capacity for suffering, as man: that does not do away with the problem, but it lessens it. Secondly, sympathy, the desire to co-suffer, seems to be found in some of the animals which man has " reclaimed." It is the function of the animal creation to minister to man; and to fulfil a proper function, even though it is not fully recognized as such, is to have some sense of fulfilment, or at least to have comfort in pain; and now that the animal creation must minister not only by serving man through its labour but by leading him to understanding through its pain, perhaps we can sometimes dimly discern some possibility of compensation in the midst of the pain. But thirdly, you find that the more primitive the human races are, the less they have of individual consciousness and the more consciousness of the group, the herd; and if this is to be verified still more of the animals then perhaps you must see the restoring function of uncomprehended suffering in this light. For the mind to find any peace in the thought of the suffering of the child you must be able to see how the child itself has its sorrow turned into joy; but if anywhere there is only the herd-consciousness, then perhaps you have some comfort and explanation in the idea—and is it impossible that animals should have some sort of instinctive awareness of it?—that the pain will bring its benefit to the herd, since it is part of that providence which is not made ineffective because of a lack of conscious apprehension of it, that providence which will in the end bring out of all this germination of (even unconscious) redemptive suffering the flowering of a new and more radiant earth.

With great labour of the mind we can, perhaps, dimly discern some sort of partial explanation of the harder aspects of the problem of pain; but how much we need the gift of the Spirit to convince the mind and bring it peace, how much we need the gift if we are to *know* that " all things work together unto good."

But then we need the gift also to enable us to live by this knowledge. Suffering can be, and is meant to be, a means to strength and to depth and clarity of vision. It is meant to be a means to love. It is meant to safeguard us against superficiality, against finding a refuge from God in the externals of religion. It is meant to show us sin as a cosmic thing, for which we share the responsibility; and therefore it is meant to lead us to the love that longs to atone and restore. We need the gift for all this: we need the gift to show us what is best to be done, how best we are to carry out God's providence; we need the strength of the gift to accept or to choose things that are costing, and to make them an expression of love, and a sharing in the redemptive sufferings of Christ. We need the gift to turn the pain that comes to us or the pain we choose into creative joy. And we need the gift, finally, to ensure that pain shall lead us, not into self-pity or complacency, not into a concentration of our own selves, but into a greater love and service of the family.

The gift of counsel is especially concerned with mercy. We shall use suffering aright if we use it to increase our pity; and we shall use it to increase our pity most fully if we use it—or rather allow the Spirit to use it in us—to increase our power to give counsel to others. The Mother of Mercy is also the Mother of Good Counsel: we must imitate her in the one as in the other. When you have learnt understanding and wisdom and the meaning of the divine pity from God's gift of pain, then you can pass on the wisdom to others, the good counsel to others, and the wisdom and the counsel will be the fine flower of pity. You will be able to minister to Christ because you will be able to speak with the voice of Christ, and so to bring to others His comfort and His strength. Unless the grain of wheat die, itself remaineth alone: you must learn through the pain of the world to be born again in the new life; but the new life is a fruitful life, fruitful for the whole world, because it ministers to Christ, it acts in and for Christ, it expresses the wisdom and the pity of the Cross. To be a man or woman of good counsel you must have learnt the christian attitude to suffering. There is something lacking even to the most brilliant mind until it has deep experience of love, and the way to that is suffering. For out of the wisdom begotten of suffering peace is born; and it is when you have peace in the depths of the soul that you can give good counsel.

We were thinking, in an earlier chapter, of the prayer of

piety, which goes beyond the prayer of awe because there is included in it the trusting familiarity of the child. Now we should think a little of the prayer of sorrow—the expression of the sense of sin and of our responsibility for the pain of the world. God is terrible. We need the prayer of sorrow to keep familiarity fearful and reverent. We need it in any case, because it is part, and a necessary part, of repentance and humility. We need it also because it is part of our redemptive pity: it is part, and a necessary part, of that acceptance of pain which restores the world. We have first to pray our sorrow for our own personal sins. Here it is important to remember that contrition is not an uncreative remorse, a brooding over the past, but a creative redeeming of the past, creative because these sins are an evil out of which good—the good of greater understanding and love— can come, and the sorrow is what thus turns them to good and so creates the future. And this creative purpose of the prayer of sorrow should determine it in practice : normally it is unwise and wasteful to go over the past in detail : and we should think rather of our general sinfulness or of the main ways in which sinfulness has been expressed in us; only when a clearer vision shows us more adequately an evil which hitherto we had treated lightly should we, normally speaking, make it the special material of our thought and prayer, so that it too may be turned more completely, by being more completely repented of, to future good.

But then, too, we must pray our sorrow for all the sin of the world, because of our share of responsibility for it. We should pray our sorrow for the original sin as well, for in this too we are all implicated. The essence of all the evil in the universe is the attempt of the creature to repudiate its dependence and become a god : the only way in which the evil can be overcome and turned into good is by reversing this movement and reasserting our creatureliness : and this we can only do by repentance and sorrow.

It is first and foremost the sin as such that we must be sorry for, the offence against God; but also we must not forget the suffering it causes; and here the prayer of sorrow turns into the prayer of pity: "They have no wine." The beauty of the world is ravaged, the purity sullied, the joy quenched, the harmony destroyed: it is in part my fault, and at least I must pray my sorrow, that to some extent I may undo the evil, and the earth to some extent may be restored. We can never return to the earthly paradise; there are some things that can never be changed however long the world goes on; but at least I can take the pain that is given me or the pain I choose and turn them into loving sorrow and into the prayer of sorrow and so increase a little the renewed sanctification and blessing, and the joy, of the world.

"If any man minister to me, let him follow me; and where I am there also shall my minister be." If we are to minister the divine pity through our sorrow we must follow: and where will He be? He will be wherever there is need of pity and good counsel: He will be in the dark places of the world, He will be where there is squalor and suffering and stupidity and sin. And how shall we be able to follow? We shall follow only if we are like Him men of sorrow and acquainted with infirmity, filled with the sense of our own sin as He was filled with the sense of the sin of all the world. But if, then, we use our power to follow Him, and follow wherever He goes, then, ministering His mercy we shall ourselves obtain mercy; giving good counsel we shall ourselves be made wise; healing others we shall ourselves be healed; for our sorrow will bring mercy and joy to our own selves, but to the self in the greatest and widest sense of the word: to the self as living in union with the whole universe of which it is a part, so that we shall know the redemptive power of pity because, in the renewal of the soul by Christ, we shall know ourselves to be a part of that universal process whereby the omnipotent pity makes all things new.

B. THE SACRAMENT OF THE
LAST ANOINTING

Amen, amen I say to thee, when thou wast younger thou didst gird thyself and didst walk where thou wouldst. But when thou shalt be old thou shalt stretch forth thy hands and another shall gird thee and lead thee whither thou wouldst not . . . And when he had said this he saith to him, Follow me.

JOHN XXI. 18, 19.

The account of the Church's custody of the energy of good in the world, its divine power to heal and sanctify and bless, is not complete until we have thought of this sacrament of the last anointing. Its purpose is to strengthen us in the last great crisis, the last great turning-point, of life; and we think of it as the sacrament of old age, when strength and vitality are at their lowest ebb and death, and the unknown life, are very near. But we cannot be too strong or too full of vitality to learn a lesson from the theology of the sacrament.

We are told that it has a fourfold purpose. It frees the mind from the trouble and fright that attend the thought of the coming of death; it heals the body if a renewal of health be for our good; it purifies the soul of sin; and it takes away to greater or less extent the weakness of soul and the need of punishment, of purgation, which sin has caused. so it is described as *consummatium totius vitae christianae,* as what brings the whole christian life to a completion, because if health is, in fact, not to be restored this sacrament immediately disposes us for the "entry into glory."

Death is the last and greatest crisis; but it should be a completion of something, not a termination; it should be a stage in the total story, a beginning rather than an end. The *Ite, missa est* of the priest at Mass is less an end than a beginning: you have received the life and the power, and

137

now you must go forth into the world and begin the redemptive work of the day. And in the same way the coming of death to the christian should be an *Ite, missa est*: you have received the life and the power, and the constant mercy of God throughout your life has brought you slowly nearer and nearer to complete possession by, and oneness with, the indwelling Trinity, and now in the last anointing the process is consummated, and so you are ready to go forth and begin the *vita nuova,* the radiant life of the eternal day.

That is why the death of holy people is a cause for rejoicing, even though we are sad because they are gone from us. And if we lived as the saints live, then we should meet death as they meet it, with a smile of welcome and joy—joy because they know that what awaits them is the completion of life, the consummation of all happiness, the fulfilment of all desire, the mercy that gives more even than they were able to desire : the glory of the infinite life and beatitude of the One. And we who are not holy can still learn something of the spirit of the saints : we shall be sad because of the littleness of our faith, we shall be frightened because of the greatness of our sin; but there is the sacrament to console and strengthen us. Remember the symbolism : it is the body that is anointed with oil for strength as for a journey (and so the vague intuition, and the longing, that are in the rites of the ancient religions are fulfilled), for the body is not done with, there is the resurrection to follow in the fullness of time; we go to a new life, but not as a man going to a new city who must leave behind him all that he loved in the old, for we go to the abidingness of the eternal present in which the Beauty we all too dimly loved and desired on earth is to take us for ever to Himself. And if we cannot have the perfect joy of the saints, still we can have something of their trust, if we have tried our best to live in love. "They shall obtain mercy " : we shall know our need of it then, but if we have tried we shall not need to be frightened.

If we have tried—that is why it is good for us to think of

this sacrament now, when perhaps death seems very remote from us. We shall be sad then because of the lost opportunities of serving God, the failures in responding to His life and power, the lack of understanding of His ways and His purposes, the sinking back into the rut of mediocre routine. We shall be sad, too, because of our failure to accept with joy the pain and drudgery of life that might have served the family and so been turned into the gold of love. We shall be sad, above all, if we have failed to minister the divine pity and mercy, for then we shall realize, as never before, our own need.

It is good to think of this now because it can help us now. The effect of this sacrament, we are told, depends on the disposition of him who receives it; but our disposition then is determined by our life here and now. And one of the things we should remember in this connection is that though final perseverance is a gift, we can do something to prepare ourselves in the hope of receiving it. It is not too difficult to love God for a day or a week or a year; but we have to prepare precisely for the *diuturnitas* of the good life—precisely for the difficulty of going on day by day until the end. You remember how Peter, immediately after those words of our Lord which told him of the death he should die, "turning about, saw that disciple whom Jesus loved," and he said "Lord, and what shall this man do?" And "Jesus saith to him, So I shall have him to remain till I come, what is it to thee? Follow thou me." For the one, death is soon to come; for the other, there is the long wait—and how agonizingly long for this "disciple whom Jesus loved." To think of this last crisis in life is to remind ourselves that we have to be prepared for the two things, for "You know not when the lord of the house cometh, at even or at midnight or at the cock-crowing or in the morning": we have to be prepared to meet death soon and suddenly, we have to be prepared to work on and on, until the even or the midnight.

The first thing, then, is to put ourselves into the hands of providence, to fashion our wills into identity with the will of the lord of the house, and accept whatever length of life He may have ordained for us. Then we must set ourselves to be in readiness. That must mean, primarily, to learn to live always in the eternal present; but it means, also, a training in patience and perseverance. We must not, of course, confuse dryness with death of soul: it is not whether we always feel joy in serving that matters, but whether we always serve. But there is the danger that sooner or later we may find the will growing tired and relaxing its efforts and so slipping into that lukewarmness of which we were thinking before. The heart that has turned to God may turn away again if its love grows cool: it may be distracted by the pleasant things of life—distracted because it isolates them from its worship of God, and tries to enjoy them for themselves alone. It may fall into self-deception, and find an interest in godly things but not for the love of God, as a man's purely aesthetic interest in the liturgy, let us say, may appear to him as a service of God though in fact it is an escape from Him. It may take refuge from the thought of God in ceaseless activity, even though it be a beneficent and religious activity. There are times when we need a will of iron, not to save us from a conscious turning away from God and the things of God, but to save us from unconsciously trying to lose our sense of God in a whirl of what would otherwise be praiseworthy activity.

"Another shall gird thee." We need patience to meet the special trials, the weakness and powerlessness, of old age; but we need patience, also, to meet the similar trials that may come upon us at any age: the sorrow of seeing our labours destroyed and we unable to prevent it; the sorrow of seeing our labours fruitless and our dreams unfulfilled; the hardness of having to watch others reap what we have sown; the hardness of having to realize that we have tried for so many years to be good christians and yet have made so little observable progress: all these things can give us a sense of powerlessness and therefore of impatience and perhaps a sort of despair. Then we have to draw ourselves back to the thought of the eternal present, the thought of the loving providence of the divine wisdom which disposes all things sweetly; we have to try to teach ourselves all over again to care and not to care, to learn to prepare for the future by making what use we can of each present moment as it comes, and leaving the rest, without worry, to the mercy of God.

" If any man minister to me, let him follow me." To learn to follow our Lord in His journey of mercy through the world is to learn to live with Him; and to learn to live with Him is to be ready to die. For it is to be steeped in the thought of His pity; and that is a thought which drives out fear. You find, indeed, in the Gospels that it is these two themes which are constantly recurring : to follow Christ, and to be without fear. Again and again our Lord says to them " Fear not, it is I." If you always try to follow and minister His mercy you need not be afraid; for He will always be there and always be saying " Fear not, it is I." God is terrible, and you must pray every day the prayer of sorrow. But He is also the Divine Pity; and if you try to follow Him every day as best you can, and have the will to go on trying to follow Him so long as He may will you to remain, then you must have a humble confidence as well. " They shall obtain mercy."

The Gospel life of Peter begins with the summons to follow his Master; and it is with the same summons, Follow me, that his life in the Gospel ends. The same is true of every christian; who is summoned and empowered to follow through the grace of baptism, and anointed with oil for the journey at confirmation, and given the daily bread of strength in the eucharist; and at the end the summons will come again. It is right that we should pray every day for the grace to be spared a sudden and unprovided death; but even this we must try to leave to His will. For the essential thing is to fear His justice, but to lift up our hands to His mercy, to sorrow and struggle but to trust; and so, at the end, if we have really tried to follow always and not to flag He will tell us to follow Him once again, but to follow Him this time with joy to His eternal dwelling, to the glory and light and peace of the everlasting hills.

CHAPTER VIII

CLEANNESS OF HEART

Blessed are the clean of heart, for they shall see God.

MATT. V. 8.

WE have been thinking of the definition of happiness, first in terms of things that you have, riches, comfort, and so on; then in terms of things that you do, the active life; there remains the question of the contemplative life, the life of vision. This, St. Thomas explains, is not to be found in the first half of any of the beatitudes since it is not the condition of acquiring happiness but is itself happiness. What you do find in these last two beatitudes is those effects of the life of action which immediately dispose a man to the life of vision; and they are two: there is that quality whereby a man is made perfect in himself for the life of vision, and there is that whereby he is made perfect in his relations with his fellow-men. The first of the two is cleanness of heart.

Let us think, to begin with, of what this means in the context of the moral life. We are concerned with the virtue of temperateness; and once again the word has become attenuated and degraded in our modern speech, and the nature of the virtue seriously misunderstood. It is not synonymous with total abstention from alcohol; it is not, in any case, restricted to a right use of food and drink; and, most important, it is not simply a negative thing, a restraint, but a positive and creative quality, an essential quality of love.

Temperateness has two aspects. First of all, it is what gives the quality of humility and reverence to our attitude to material things. It is what enables us to love things in-

stead of grabbing and mauling and battening on them; it
is what enables us to contemplate and not to devour.

You can see an example of what this means—though the
example itself is not necessarily an act of the virtue of temperateness—in the reverence with which a man who is alive
to beauty will treat a glass of rare wine: the christian
virtue of temperateness differs from this because the motive
is different—not the appreciation of beauty as an end in
itself, but the curbing and training of the appetites for the
love of God and His justice and therefore the restoring of
the rule of spirit over flesh. It remains true that christian
temperateness is essentially a humility of the flesh towards
material things. As we saw in the first chapter, they are not
just means to man's pleasure; they are of value in themselves
as the handiwork of God, created to glorify Him; and so
we have to learn to love them without greed and treat them
without irreverence. Moreover, in the christian economy of
life, things have an additional dignity: they are meant to
receive a share of the blessing which flows from the redemptive power of Christ, to be, in a sense, sanctified in themselves, and so to form a part of that process of total restoration whereby the world as a whole is led back to God. (So
we say grace before meat; and so in the Church's ritual you
find a form of blessing for all the material things which
minister to the life of man.) You must treat them, then,
with additional reverence, since there is this much of holiness in them. Then thirdly, there is the thought of the
universal providence of God, so that the least of these
things which come into our lives and minister to us must
be regarded, not simply as ministering to a pleasure which
implies no further purpose or responsibility, but on the contrary as the instrument, however small, of an eternal pro-
vision for an eternal destiny, and in the end as a part of
God's eternal design for the world as a whole. And
fourthly, there is the glory of the omnipresence of God Himself in all His creatures; so that your reverence for them

must be a part of your reverence for Him who makes them His habitation.

And when you think, not of material things in general, but of the bodies of men and women, then your reverence must be immeasurably intensified. For this is the flesh which in Christ was raised to the Godhead, and which thenceforward is in itself for ever glorified; and it is the flesh in which the Godhead, the indwelling Trinity, resides in a special and intimate sense, so that those who have this presence within them are really one with the Godhead they adore, and therefore to treat them with irreverence is to be irreverent to God.

But you can only learn this christian reverence for creatures by learning the second aspect of temperateness; the body needs to be chastised and beaten into subjection; to be temperate is to have learnt, not indeed to kill desires, but to control them. Here the virtue involves a constant daily discipline, a constant denial of the autonomous desires of the senses in order to affirm the rule of the spirit over a unified personality. Temperateness, and all the virtues which are part of it or connected with it, chastity, sobriety, gentleness, modesty and the rest, train and subdue the passions of man so that instead of being masters enslaving the soul they may become what they are intended by God to be, a part of the total unified drive which is man's journey to God.

It is temperateness which makes us reverent; and thus it is not temperateness but its opposite which is negative, and implies a lack of being. If you lack temperateness you lack reverence, and therefore you cannot love. And this lack you suffer whenever you grab and domineer and do violence. You cannot love, you are restricted to a partial, because selfish and sensual, pleasure; whereas love is a total enhancement of being, a glorifying of the whole body-spirit, because it is essentially a vital oneness with what is good and lovely. Temperateness, therefore, safeguards and per-

fects the life of the senses and therefore of the whole personality; for the purpose of the life of the senses is to enable
us to know and love and become one with God's creatures
and through them to be led to God—all God's creatures, but
human beings especially—and so to have our own being
immeasurably enlarged. Whereas intemperateness is the
denial of this enlargement of being, because the refusal of
reverence means the refusal to regard things as objects of
love (with the measure of equality and reciprocity which all
love implies) and to substitute for this relationship of two-
in-unity a purely one-sided utilization. It is because it is
purely one-sided that there is no enlargement of being: the
self remains enclosed completely in its own narrow selfhood;
and as long as it is intemperate, as long as it refuses to learn
to be reverent, it can never break its bonds.

The intemperate man thus does a threefold violence: to
himself, his own nature, since he is made to love and therefore to be made whole; to creatures as things in themselves,
worthy of reverence and contemplation and love; to God
who gives this value to creatures and is present with them
and loves what He has made. To be intemperate is to be a
destroyer. But to be temperate is not to destroy but to fulfil.
It is not to destroy passion or the delight of the senses in
material things, but to fulfil them by fulfilling their nature.
You do not love less, but more, when you treat them
reverently as the wine-lover treats his wine. You do not love
less, but more, when your passion is ordered and controlled
by reverence, for then it is glorified and intensified by being
the vehicle of the life and power of Spirit; and you turn it
into what, of its very nature, it is intended to be: an organic
element in the total process of enlargement of the whole
body-spirit, a means to the forging of the oneness of two
beings, and a part of the shared life of love and worship and
service of God.

Temperateness, then, is first of all the condition of the
deep personal union of the self with other beings. But it is
more than that. If the greatest reason for your reverence

is your sense of God's presence in creatures, if you have learnt thus to see things aright by seeing God within them, then you learn to make your whole life a unity, you learn to make your life not an agglomerate of unconnected interests but a single and all-inclusive fire, you learn to make all desires the different aspects and expressions of a single desire, the desire to serve God. Then you will be clean of heart, and fit to see God, because you will have learnt to love nothing apart from Him; you will be clean of heart, and fit to see God, because by restoring its function to the life of the senses and making it a harmonious element in the total life of the body-spirit (not destroying the body to liberate the soul, but liberating the body from the separateness of lust and greed that it may really be the partner of the soul) you will yourself have achieved integrity, wholeness, and so restored something at least of the power of vision. And you will be a little worthy of the life of heaven because you will incidentally have achieved beauty : that "shining forth of spirit through matter " which transforms and glorifies matter—the shining and transforming beauty which you find always in the face of the saints.

You will have achieved, also, that purity of mind which is the second meaning of cleanness of heart. For the four cardinal virtues are, in a sense, aspects of all virtuous action : there is a temperateness of the mind which corresponds to the temperateness of the flesh, a temperateness in regard to truth. You are intemperate if you do violence to truth by trying to make it simply a means to your profit or pleasure; you are intemperate if you twist and pervert it. All the forms of wishful thinking and self-deception, all the ways in which you compromise and whittle away the truth, every lack of candour—to yourself, to other men, to God— all these things are forms of intemperateness of mind. So are the ways in which we do violence in our thought to the nature of divinity : the anthropomorphisms, the projections on to the divine nature of human emotions and limitations, the tendency to forget the justice of God and the need of awe in face of the terrible and to take refuge in a sentimental and humanitarian picture of His mercy. Intemperate, too, are the debased sentimental forms of piety and worship: the ways in which we turn worship into a sort of self-indulgence, pandering to emotions instead of lifting them up into a total act of worship of the whole body-spirit which both expresses and strengthens the will, and fixes the gaze not on ourselves but on the reality of God. And indeed you find in this self-indulgent parody of worship the same elements of irreverence and selfishness and sensuality that you find in the intemperateness of the flesh. Instead of enhancement of the whole being you have the isolated and therefore self-destructive indulgence of a part of the being; instead of a relationship of love you have the isolation of the soul in its own selfhood, and the attempt to treat God as a utility; instead of the oneness with all creation which is in true worship you have the ignoring of everything but the desires of the self. This is the way, not to cleanness of heart, but from it; it is the negation of vision, for you are not concerned to look at anything but to indulge yourself; you make the heart blind and opaque and gross because you make it turgid and muddy—like repository art.

We can see the way to cleanness of heart, on the other hand, if we look at the Church's liturgy, for indeed if its first and supreme purpose is to give worship to God, it has the additional purpose of cleansing the mind and heart and the whole personality. Rather we should say that its purpose is to cleanse the personality so that then we may be able to offer God a more adequate sharing in the worship of Christ. The liturgy is art; but its essential material is man himself. The various arts of man, and all the creatures of the earth, and the sun and moon and stars, are brought into the act of worship; but it is first and foremost the total man (in Christ) who is self-offered, the total man who is expressed, the total man who is cleansed.

For the liturgy is both the revealing expression of the divine reality and man's response to it; and as the reality is expressed in sensible form and symbol, in rational statement, and in terms of the good which calls to the heart, so the response is the total response of senses, intuition, reason and feeling (including in feeling both the emotions and the will). Song and gesture and movement are the body's part in the total self-offering; and that offering includes the response of all the senses to the reality expressed. Life is given to this outward worship by the offering of mind and heart, raised to God in and through it; and again that self-offering of spirit includes the response of reason to the rational formulae of faith, of intuition to their symbolic expression, of emotion and will to those other aspects of the truth which we call the good and the beautiful.

But in the offering and expression of the total man the total man is also cleansed. The liturgy is sacramental art : it effects what it signifies. This is, of course, true primarily of the sacraments themselves; but it is true in a broader sense of the whole of the liturgy : the evoking of this response from the worshipper is itself a purification of the worshipper, and a process whereby he is assimilated to the reality revealed. Think of some very simple example : the lighted candle, for instance, which is part of so much of the Church's worship. There is food there for reason, for endless meditation : we know that the candle expresses worship, and the worship of love; it expresses the single-mindedness of the true christian, whose whole life is to be an ascending flame of worship to God; we need not neglect the utilitarian aspect of the flame, for its purpose is to give light to other things than itself, and so is ours (we remember that it was said of the Baptist, he was a burning and shining light); and the candle is carried for the reading of the Gospel, which is the Light expressed in words, the words of the Word who is Light eternal; and our worship will be whole, and useful to the world, when it is wholly united with the self-offering of that same light which shines in the darkness. With all this and much more we can fill the reasoning mind; and in so filling it we purify it, we give direction to all the other thoughts which will follow when the moment of worship is over, and, if we are faithful, turn them also into worship. But what reasoning can thus work out step by step, intuition can seize immediately, more dimly, perhaps, but more deeply: I am to be that candle; I am to be light and fire in Christ. And there follows the upward movement of will and desire and feeling, for this Godward movement is, in fact, the fulfilment of the heart's perhaps unrecognised desire, and therefore is felt as good and desirable and to be achieved; and so it is that the symbolism of the liturgy can work in us even unconsciously, even if rationally we do not understand it: it can form the soul to its own pattern, until in the end the pattern is expressed in the life of thought and action. And finally the senses themselves are purified and perfected: you cannot live constantly with debased art without running the risk of being yourself debased, unless your awareness and your criticism ceaselessly react against it; you cannot live constantly with this God-revealing art without yourself being turned gradually into worship; and the burning light and the tall white cylinder of wax, the purity of form and purpose, are a purgation for vision muddied by other appeals in which matter is isolated from spirit and degraded, and therefore turned to negation.

The liturgy is the worship of the total man; it is also and above all the worship of the *totus Christus,* the total Christ, in whom the voice of all creation speaks. The liturgy is cosmic art. The reality revealed is the answer to the age-old dreams of the universe, of that creation which is in travail even till now; and again it is both a response and offering and a cleansing, for this returning of the universe to the Life is itself a renewal of life, a healing and sanctifying and blessing. So, if you learn through the Church's liturgy to be clean of heart you do three things: you achieve a personal integrity through a worship which is neither rational nor emotional but total, and therefore a total renewal of the self; you recover something of the integrity of the self in the cosmic family, and share in some degree in the bringing back of the cosmos to its Source; you respond to that divine power which will give you the essential integrity without which nothing else is of importance: the integrity of the self in the infinity of God.

"They shall see God." To the gift of the Spirit which, working indeed not least through our reverent response to the liturgy, gives us a far deeper penetration and clarity of mind, we must turn later; but let us here remember what will then be more emphatically verified: that to be clean of heart is to be as a child, to have the clearness of eye of the child and the reverent docility towards reality that goes with it. Unless you are willing to accept reality as it is, and to reverence it for what it is, you cannot be clean of heart and mind. We have, therefore, to pray for that docility; we have to pray for that detachment and meekness and mourning, the hunger for God's justice and the power of pity, may all together give us that temperateness towards things and towards truth which will recover for us our power of vision, and so make us fit for the Vision. It is more to see God, says St. Thomas, than to sit at His table; "just as he is the greater man at court who not only dines but sees the king's countenance." Self-centredness, and the lust which expresses it, make us blind and take the life from us; if we want to be happy we must learn to see God and His creatures as they are in themselves, and for their own sakes: we must pray all our lives the prayer of the man in the Gospel: "Lord, that I may see."

Now it came to pass, when he drew nigh to Jericho, that a certain blind man sat by the wayside begging. And he cried out, saying, Jesus Son of David have mercy on me . . . And Jesus asked him, saying : What wilt thou that I do to thee ? But he said : Lord that I may see. Jesus said to him : Receive thy sight ; thy faith hath made thee whole. And immediately he saw and followed him, glorifying God.

LUKE XVIII. 35-43.

St. Paul when he is writing to the Corinthians, makes a sharp distinction between the wisdom of this world and the wisdom of the Spirit. " It is written," he says, " *I will destroy the wisdom of the wise*. . . . For the foolishness of God is wiser than men; and the weakness of God is stronger than men. . . . The foolish things of the world hath God chosen that he may confound the wise : and the weak things of the world hath God chosen that He may confound the strong." And again he says, " We speak the wisdom of God in a mystery, a wisdom which is hidden . . . which none of the princes of this world knew. For if they had known it, they would never have crucified the lord of glory." And when he is speaking of the unknown things that God has prepared for those that love Him, he says, " But to us God hath revealed them, by his Spirit. For the Spirit searcheth all things, yea the deep things of God."*

We are not to suppose that St. Paul is here setting the wisdom which is " from above " in opposition to such wisdom as men can acquire by the right use of the mind, as though the two things were incompatible. It is not these two which are incompatible. In the great saints who were also great thinkers you can distinguish four wisdoms: philosophy, theology, faith, and the wisdom which comes

* 1 Cor. i and ii.

directly from the Spirit; they are distinct, they are different
kinds of wisdom, but they do not clash. St. Paul is speaking
of those who are "wise according to the flesh," of the
"princes of *this* world" (which again in the Gospel sense
is the world of darkness of Satan, of Mammon and pride),
of the "sensual man." In other words, we have here simply
an application of that general contrast we have been considering all along: the world unredeemed and therefore
still in the power of evil and darkness, the self which tries
to be independent of God; and, on the other hand, the world
redeemed and therefore repentant and docile to the Spirit
and receptive of the power of the Spirit, the self which has
been re-born and has the Life within it, and can learn the
truth from the Truth.

Philosophy, in this new life, does not lose its glory; but
part of its glory is to recognize its limitations, and admit
that there are mysteries it can never fathom. Faith and
theology can tell us immeasurably more; and the things they
tell us are immeasurably more important; but even so we
see "as in a glass darkly," for the object of faith is in itself
obscure: it is not yet the vision face to face to which it
aspires. And so the deeper wisdom is given to those who are
docile enough to receive it; and the mind which can be
quickened by the Spirit pierces—not by direct vision indeed
but by a vital experience—even to the profundities of God,
non solum discens sed et patiens divina: not only learning
about the things of God but actually living them in the
depths of the heart.

So St. Thomas tells us that this understanding is an
"intimate knowledge," for in two ways it differs from abstract rational knowledge: it pierces to the heart of things,
and it is itself the heart's knowledge, the knowledge that
is born of love. How can love be said to know? Because
when a thing is loved it becomes in a special sense, as the
old theologians used to say, "connatural" to the lover: it
is immediately *experienced*. You know a great deal *about*
the thing you love, but if you put down on paper all that

you thus know you do not really touch on the essential, precisely because the essential is something that will not be put down in rational terms. Love is rightly said to know because the experience which is love becomes a part of the object, and so the mind knows the object precisely as loved and as experienced. You know the same thing, but you know it in a different way. You are beyond the realm of knowledge about things: you are in the realm of that *connaissance toute cordiale,* that knowledge of the heart, which, because it is a direct experience, is a union not only of mind with its object but of the whole being with the thing loved.

When you apply this to the things of faith its importance is obvious. We know as in a glass darkly; we know much about God through the mercy of His self-revelation, but this revelation is necessarily expressed for us in human terms, the terms of the creeds and doctrinal formularies. We are still obliged, therefore, to know the Creator through created things, created words. Because of this inadequacy, because of the immeasurable distance between this human expression of the reality and the reality itself, there arises, first of all, the danger of error and false interpretations; and secondly there is the inevitable dissatisfaction of the mind which always aspires to vision. "I sought Him whom my soul loveth: I sought Him and I found Him not." So the gifts of the Spirit are given, to overcome in some degree the obscurity of faith.

We are not yet concerned with the gift of wisdom, which takes the soul straight to the (still hidden) Godhead. The gift of knowledge enables us to judge—not by a process of reasoning but by a sort of inspired experience, so that a man feels rather than judges the truth of his conclusions—about what is and is not to be believed. Now we are concerned with understanding: that God-given experience which penetrates to the depths of the mysteries as revealed to us in human terms. And the first way in which this is achieved shows us the connection between this gift and the quality of cleanness of heart.

The discipline of philosophy consists in training the mind to see and investigate immaterial reality without being misled by sensory images; and in the same way the drawing near of the mind to God demands an emancipation from the sensory images, the anthropomorphisms, which must otherwise lead it astray. "We shall know God the more perfectly in this life," says St. Thomas, "in so far as we understand more and more how He surpasses everything the intellect can comprehend." It is, of course, essential to distinguish between this *via negativa* of the men of prayer—the setting aside, when searching for God in prayer, of all distraction from sensory images, from created reality, in order to arrive at the cloud of unknowing in which the Godhead itself is sensed—from the way of rejection as a total attitude to life. As a christian, as we have seen, you are inevitably concerned with created things: you are part of the world that God has made, and you have a duty towards it; you cannot love God if you refuse to love your neighbour. But here we are concerned, not with our attitude to the world, but with the question of how to pray; and it is clear that if we are to set our minds to searching for God we must first try to free them, for the time of prayer, from all those things which would impede them in their quest: the cares, anxieties, preoccupations of our daily life in general, and in particular the sensory images which must misrepresent the Godhead. "When thou shalt pray," our Lord tells us, "enter into thy chamber and, having shut the door, pray to thy Father in secret." He is speaking primarily against ostentation; but His words are also the perfect symbol of this ascent of the soul to God. "We must remember," says St. John of the Cross, "that the Word the Son of God, together with the Father and the Holy Ghost, is hidden in essence and presence in the inmost being of the soul. The soul, therefore, that will find Him must go out from all things in will and affection and enter into the profoundest self-recollection, and all things must be to it as if they existed not. Hence St. Augustine saith: 'I found

Thee not without, O Lord; I sought Thee without in vain, for Thou are within.' . . . Seeing, then, that the Bridegroom whom thou lovest is the treasure hidden in the field of thy soul, for which the wise merchant gave all that he had, so thou, if thou wilt find Him, must forget all that is thine, withdraw from all created things, and hide thyself in the secret retreat of the spirit, shutting the door upon thyself—that is, denying thy will in all things—and praying to thy Father in secret. Then thou, being hidden within Him, wilt be conscious of His presence in secret, and wilt love Him, possess Him in secret, and delight in Him in secret, in a way that no tongue or language can express."

Happy, then, are the clean of heart because, in the first place, they have learnt to reverence all things in and for God, so that their minds and hearts are not always being led away from God but, on the contrary, are always being drawn to Him. Happy, in the second place, because they can be led by the Spirit into this secret place apart and be undistracted by senses and imaginings, and so can learn to search even the profundities of God.

To be undistracted, unperturbed: you find in theologians and mystics alike a constant emphasis on the idea of *quiet*. The gift of understanding, the theologians tell us, gives the soul a sense of the certitude of the things of faith, a sense of the inner meaning of the scriptural account of the divine mysteries, a sense of the infinite perfection of God and the nothingness of man, which bring it *quiet*. And the mystics describe the effects of this gift precisely in terms of the " prayer of quiet." "There came to me in this *quiet*," says St. Teresa, "the delightful discovery of the hidden sense in the Psalms and the Scriptures." And again: "The soul then receives communication concerning the great truths . . .; without seeing the Master so full of kindness who teaches her, she *knows that He is near her*." It is that quiet sense of the near presence of Him in whom are all things, and the quiet sense of certitude which the presence brings, that this gift establishes in the prayerful soul. That is why it is so immensely important that we should set aside some time every day—half an hour if we can possibly manage it, a quarter of an hour at the very least—for the purpose of learning to pray thus in secret, learning to be quiet in the presence, and so to acquire all through the day a "sense of our last end."

We have been thinking, previously, of the prayer of awe, the prayer of filial reverence, the prayer of petition, the prayer of sorrow. Here we come to the lovely prayer of wonder : the still, wordless gaze of adoration which is proper to the lover. You are not talking, not busy, not worried or agitated : you are not asking anything : you are *quiet,* you are just *being with,* and there is love and wonder in your heart. So this prayer is indeed a beginning of beatitude; for the heart is filled and is content simply to be—and its being is all adoration. You find some hint of this utterly serene but utterly humble sense of infinity in some of the greatest music : in some of Bach or of César Franck, for example, or of the Beethoven of the last quartets, or again in Wolf's *Ganymed.* You find it in the music of the Mass, when the *alleluia* traces its pattern of sound on the last vowel, saying nothing yet saying everything. You find it expressed in the words of the apostle Thomas, abashed at his unbelief : My Lord and my God.

But let us note three points of great importance. First, this is a prayer to which we must aspire; but the way of prayer is long and hard, and we have to begin at the beginning. Nor should we suppose that only this prayer of quiet can give us a constant sense of God's presence, and of our last end : any sincere prayer will gradually do that, though the prayer of quiet will do it more forcibly and more fully. Secondly, the prayer of quiet will never supersede the simplicities of the *Our Father* : we never get beyond the need of awe and fear and sorrow and petition. This prayer may be given to us at moments, and if we grow in wisdom the moments will be longer and more frequent; that is all. And thirdly, it is true that in the prayer of quiet you ask nothing, you simply adore; but this adoration is never an indifference to the fate of the world, of your brethren : you shut the door and pray in secret, you " forget all that is yours and withdraw from all created things " that the mind and heart may leap up to God; but because you have charity in you the needs and sorrows of these created things go silently with you, they are part of you, and the blessings with which you return is a blessing in which they must necessarily share. Your love of God still includes your love of your family.

And indeed, as we saw in the last section, it is precisely this same sort of attitude which the virtue of temperateness teaches us to adopt towards all created things, as part of our reverence for God. For them, too, you must learn to feel wonder, provided always that you guard yourself against isolating their beauty from its Maker. And here, too, perhaps the gift of understanding has its purpose : since it can teach us to go to the heart of things and to learn the heart's knowledge even where no beauty is apparent, even where there is stupidity and sin. It can teach us to go beyond a perhaps unattractive, perhaps repulsive exterior, to the presence of God within; it can teach us to reverence the pain and the ugliness of the world, for in these, too, is implicit the love-mercy of God.

It can, therefore, lead us to the prayer of gratitude. There are problems which only the heart's knowledge, piercing to the heart of things where God's pity abides, can solve; and to solve them is to be grateful to God, for the solution is the pity. And this prayer, too, at its highest and best is part of the wordless prayer of wonder and adoration, for the deepest wonder is aroused not simply by Beauty in itself, but by Beauty stooping to comfort ugliness because of the pity which is love.

The prayer of wonder is not, like the prayer of petition, primarily a means to something : it is an end in itself, it is life, and the beginning of beatific life. But you cannot pray this prayer without its overflowing into action, the sort of action that saves and heals and consoles. And because of the twofold meaning of cleanness of heart the converse is also true: the more your service of the world grows in reverence and love, the more the virtue of temperateness draws your love of all things into the unity of your love of God, so also the more you will grow in clearness of heart's knowledge and therefore in wonder, the more you will be made worthy to see and praise God in the final fulfilment of vision of the heavenly home.

B. THE SACRAMENT OF MARRIAGE

And the wine failing, the mother of Jesus saith to him : They have no wine. . . . Jesus saith to them : Fill the waterpots with water. And they filled them up to the brim.

JOHN II. 3. 7.

Christianity is the creed of acceptance. You must not dally with manicheism, the *pessima haeresis* : you must never think that some of the things that God has made are good and to be accepted while others are evil in themselves. The gracious miracle at Cana is our Lord's affirmation of the goodness of material things: His approval of wine and gaiety and good-fellowship. His approval of the vocation of marriage. They filled them up to the brim; the first thing is to accept the gift of life with both hands from God; and that includes the full acceptance of human nature, of the unity of the body-spirit.

But there is also the other side. To be a full acceptance of life it must be an acceptance, also, of the fact of sin. You accept the wholeness of human nature and its essential goodness; but you realize that sin has twisted it and turned it to evil. And so you have to safeguard your affirmation from becoming an idolatry; and you have, in particular, to safeguard your joy in material things from becoming

isolated from the governance of the spirit. Material things
are to be reverenced for what they are; they are not just
utilities; but, on the other hand, it is part of their nature
to fulfil a function and it is part of the reverence we owe
to them to remember that function.

Sex in man is essentially different from sex in animals,
because its function is different. It is not a purely biological
thing : it is much greater than that. Of its nature it is also
part of that process whereby the oneness of two human
beings is achieved; and that oneness itself is meant to be a
means whereby the two human beings together become one
with God. Human marriage is the most complete fulfilment of the part the body may play in the union of spirit
with spirit, and may thus become, too, the ground of the
union of this two-in-unity with infinite Spirit.

They filled them up to the brim. There is nothing niggardly or half-hearted about this christian acceptance of
the flesh; and the acceptance of the body's function is the
acceptance of the fullness of human love. But as we have
seen, you need the virtue of temperateness, not to deny or
destroy, but, on the contrary, to fulfil : and you fulfil precisely in so far as you avoid both idolatry and sensuality by
making sex part of the totality of love, and love part of the
totality of worship.

Man is essentially a creator. Married love is normally the
primary fulfilment of men and women because normally it
is the primary form of creation. " And the Lord God said :
It is not good for man to be alone." The individual is incomplete : incomplete in body and mind and heart and
will; and in the normal way of things it is through the love
of men and women for each other that that manifold completeness comes. And the creation of new life is both the
expression of that completeness (for now it is the new thing,
the new unity, which is creative and outward-turning) and
also the means whereby the completeness is achieved (for
the unity not only of the flesh but of mind and heart as well
is made through this making). Similarly with the worship

of God : it is the two who are now one who express and glorify their oneness in worship; but worship is also the highest means whereby their oneness is established and made eternally secure.

Christianity, then, so far from condemning sex or regarding it as something shameful or something to be apologized for, raises it, together with the whole man of whom it is a function, to a new dignity : first, inasmuch as it is an element in the normal means whereby men and women are to worship God in fullness of life; secondly, because it is part of that vocation of marriage which our Lord has raised to the dignity of a sacrament, with all that that implies of supernatural greatness. To that greatness we shall return in a moment; let us first of all think of the sacrament in terms of the special needs it is destined to meet. Marriage is a great vocation, is indeed the normal human vocation; but a vocation is a life-work, and to think of it in these terms is, therefore, to be on our guard against romanticizing it and forgetting its true nature. It is a lifework because it is something which takes a lifetime to achieve. You have first of all the making of the unity of man and woman; and this is itself an endless process. On the physical level there is need of gentle adjustment of the two wills that there may be real peace and fulfilment; in the sphere of mind there is the long and laborious process, not indeed of coming to agree on every conceivable issue, but of reaching a real and stable sympathy of mind, a real unity on great issues, a real mutual complementing of the two different ways of thought; finally there has to be the unity of the deep personal will, not again that there can ever be a complete agreement of desire in every superficial and transient issue, but that beneath the surface-differences there may be a solid core of unity which nothing can shake. All this is not achieved in a day or a year. Nor is the making of the family, and of the life of the family, which is both the purpose of the unity of man and woman and the means to it. And here, especially, we have to be careful not to roman-

D.P.   F ticize: the stuff of married life is the daily work, the daily drudgery; all the burdens which the care of children involves; the economic anxieties; the responsibilities; and finally the selflessness which knows and accepts the time when the unity of the family has to be split up, and the new generation must go forth and make its own life and its own families. Unless all this can be recognized as the essence of marriage there is bound to be disaster. There is the deep, underlying joy, there is the long happiness of comradeship, there are the moments of glory; these, too, are essential, for they are love, and it is love which turns drudgery into joy. But if you try to isolate the glamour and forget the labour, if you think of marriage as an endless, care-free honeymoon, then you are distorting its nature, and you will be very unhappy. That is the first reason why we are given this sacrament: to help us to make marriage a *life*, a life in which the hard work is never eluded but fully accepted, and turned by the power of love into something creative—the creation of goodness and happiness, to the creation of worship.

They filled them up to the brim. When you accept the reality of marriage thus with both hands and in its wholeness, and refuse to deceive yourself into thinking that glamour is all, then the power of the sacrament will make your love strong and lasting and the means of a closer and closer union with God. It will do more than that. The family is meant to be creative of more than itself.

The first glory of parenthood is that man and woman become, in the words of a Pope, the "ministers of God's omnipotence," sharing with Him in the tremendous work of making immortal human beings. But they are also the symbol of the union of Christ and His Church: and that union, too, is a creative thing, from which the power of good in the world, and the victory of good in the world, proceed. To love together is to create worship; to worship together is to create love: but also to love and worship as one is to help in the creating of the life of the Church. The new unity looks beyond itself to the life of the family, the home; but the home, in its turn, must look beyond itself to the world without. Apply here what we have been thinking of in earlier chapters: the spirit of poverty, meekness, mourning and the rest, the spirit of loving and creative sacrifice: you have in the love which can give itself to and for the child a symbol of—and more than that, an introduction to—the sacrificial life of love of the christian in the world. The family, in its turn, must give itself to and for the world. It must be for the world a visible demonstration of the religion of love; and that it will be, first of all, by its own unity and peace; but the unity and peace must turn outward, must radiate love and light and the homage of service, so that the home may be, not only something that others can admire, but a hearth to which they can always come and be welcome, and sit, and be warm.

Marriage is thus the normal way, not only in which men and women become whole in themselves, not only in which they love and worship God, but also in which they serve the Church and the world. And those whose vocation is not to married life? They can be in a yet higher state, if they choose the life of virginity for the love of God, if the good things of family life are forgone in order to know and love and serve God more fully and more intensely. And the point that is relevant here is that the Church exalts this state of virginity not, as is too commonly supposed, because it disapproves of sex or human love or the family (it is indeed in these days almost the only surviving defender of family life), but precisely because it knows that this state of life is not a destruction of love, even of love of men, but, on the contrary, an immense enlargement and enrichment of it, a dedication to it.

Those in this state of life have their family, but it is a larger family, and one which it is harder to serve. Some are called to the family life of the cloister: they have the same need to love and to be made whole by their love; the same need to see the building up of the life of their family

as their primary life-work; the same need, therefore, to
make the good of the family the criterion of what they do;
the same need to go beyond justice, and see that the family
life is built not on the bare minimum of justice but on the
maximum of love. They lack the help of the physical love
which can be so vast a driving force for the making of the
unity of spirit; they lack the blood ties which can do so
much to make the home a unity; they have special dangers:
of order turning into starchy formalism, of authority being
degraded into external regimentation and routine, of love
being destroyed by divisions and incompatibilities and prejudices. But they have, too, their special graces; and in
addition they escape some of the dangers of the smaller
world of married life. They need not find their celibacy
a subtraction of life, a disability to mind or body, if their
energies are turned to the wider opportunities of their
family life—all the creative work of the cloister itself, but
also the creation of a wider and wider circle of love and
pity and strengthening influence in the world about
them. And as with the ordinary human home, so with the
religious house, it is as a family, as a unity of love and
worship, that it best can help in the building of the world
outside.   The individual can do much to draw men to
Christ; but when you have a whole community which is a
visible demonstration of the life of love in Christ, and of
the loving invitation of Christ, then indeed you have a
power in the land.

And still there are others whose vocation it is to live
neither a married nor a community life: they, too, have
their family, and it is immediately the world. Theirs can
be the hardest vocation of all; for they must be all things
to all men without the strength and solace of a smaller
unity to complete them and make them happy. Such, for
example, are the priests who do not live in community—
but of them we must think later on when we come to the
last of the sacraments—though clearly they, too, in a sense,
have their smaller family, the community immediately

about them in their parish, which they have to labour to build into a unity of love and worship that it in its turn may fulfil its family vocation in the greater world; and in the power of the priesthood all the labour and drudgery of making and serving that family is turned to glory. Such also are all those who give themselves in charity to a life of service of mankind—in nursing, in art, in scientific research —and to do so the more fully, deny themselves the comfort of a family life of their own.

Whether, then, you think of married life, or of these other ways in which you have always to make and serve the life of a family, the same essential truth holds good : you worship God by and in your making, and in your making you yourself become whole, and each of the three things is the cause of the others : you make well if your making is worship; you worship well if you worship as a maker; and your making and your worship are what make you whole. But the condition, too, is always the same. They filled them up to the brim : you accept your vocation in its fullness, the fullness of marriage and family life, the fullness of the shared life of any community, the fullness of a life of sacrifice to humanity as a whole, but to humanity not as an abstract but as the total family of individual men and women. Then, if your acceptance is the acceptance of love; if the drudgery is turned into an endless expression of love; if the family life you have fashioned turns outward to the larger world with all the power of love, and of love-in-unity, so that the circle of its healing influence grows wider and wider as the years go by, and the intensity of its love burns deeper and deeper, till you have conquered prejudices and limitations and your house and your heart are always full—then, indeed, you will have filled your life to the brim in love and gratitude and service to Him who is Life to every man that cometh into the world, and in the power of His universal love and universal pity He will bless you, and the water will be turned into wine.

CHAPTER IX

THE LOVE OF PEACE

Blessed are the peace-makers, for they shall be called the children of God.
MATT. V. 9.

THE quality in our relations with our fellow-men which, says St. Thomas, immediately disposes us to the life of vision is the love of peace. And why? Because the life of vision—the life of the quiet prayer of wonder and the greater prayer of union—is incompatible with agitation. You cannot adore the Other in self-oblivion, you cannot "cast all your cares away," if you are tossed about on a sea of worries and solicitudes about external things; nor can you if you are not yet at peace within the mind itself because of a lack of complete identity of will with the infinite Will. "Wisdom," says St. Augustine, "is to the peace-lovers, in whom there is no movement of rebellion, but obedience to Reason." But wisdom is the end.

It is useful for man to have much information about matters of fact; but that is not wisdom. It is useful to have scientific knowledge, to know the immediate what and why of things; but that is not wisdom either. It is better to have philosophy, which is the knowledge of things not in their immediate but in their ultimate causes: that is wisdom, though it is not the highest form of wisdom. It is wisdom because it does reduce the manifold of life to the one, and therefore makes things intelligible as a unity; but you need, to make the dry bones live, the vision, the intuition or awareness, of things in all their concreteness, their goodness and beauty as well as their truth; above all, you need some degree, at least, of direct knowledge of the nature of the one; and when you have *that* vision in its plenitude—

the plenitude which, knowing something of God in Himself, sees all things in Him and Him in all things—and at the same time the wisdom which judges all things in the light of the highest of all causes, the Cause of all being Itself, then you have wisdom in the fullest and deepest sense; and seeing things as it were with the eyes of God, you share something of the peace of God.

But that supreme wisdom, as we have seen, is "from above"; it is given to those who have the humility and the docility to receive it; it is given to those who have learnt to be as little children. Wisdom is to those who are obedient to Reason; that conformity is not a negation of freedom, a yoke upon the mind, but the liberation of the spirit from darkness into light; it is the joy and peace and exhilaration of learning from Love. It is peace, in particular, because it brings with it a security—of the will as well as of the mind —which no acquired wisdom can have. "And when they shall bring you into the synagogues and to magistrates and powers, be not solicitous how or what you shall answer, or what you shall say: for the Holy Ghost shall teach you in the same hour what you must say." You are care-free, you cannot be racked with worry, your mind is at rest, because you have the untroubled vision and the docility of the child.

Happy are the peace-makers; but you cannot be a peace-maker among your brethren unless you are also acquiring some measure of peace in your own heart. You must be trying to live in what Augustine calls the *tranquillitas ordinis*: the tranquillity which comes of ordered desire— and desires are ordered when they are unified, when all desires are aspects of one single desire, and all loves are included in one universal love. You have the tranquillity of order, in other words, when you have within you the re-integration of God's order; when you are reborn in the Spirit and so made whole, and made whole because restored to the status of a son of God. That is why the peace-lovers are happy: because they shall be called the children of God. The two things, wisdom, sonship, are related; and why? Because, says St. Thomas, it is wisdom which makes us like to Christ the Wisdom begotten of the Father. All that mediatorship in Christ which we have been thinking of as the function of the christian in the world, all the work the christian must do to heal and comfort and strengthen and restore, all depends on wisdom. Goodwill is not enough. There must be the hunger and thirst to do; but there must be the wisdom which instructs what to do.

So you come back again to the child, whose vision is not clouded by prejudice, nor his judgement twisted by the pragmatisms of selfish profit or pleasure. It is a tragedy that our art, in its representations of the Wisdom begotten of the Father, has lost the tradition of the *Puer Aeternus,* the Eternal Boy, that christian fulfilment of the conception of the youthful Apollo in his slender grace and supple strength of body, his clear and serene intellectuality, with the addition of the divine gentleness of the Shepherd. For this is the beauty that is ever old and ever new: ever old because there is in it the pitying wisdom of all the ages of the world, ever new because there is in it the gracious receptivity of youth. Christ is the eternal Wisdom, but the eternal Wisdom begotten: we become like to Him, and therefore filled with His peace, when we learn from Him the age-old wisdom by learning to be as a child.

Then if we are thus, if through docility we are learning little by little to make all desires one desire, then we are beginning also to be lovers and makers of peace in the world: not only by what we do and say but by what we are we shall beget peace in the hearts of others. This beatitude is indeed the fruit of the preceding ones: for you will give to others if you are poor in spirit and not grasping; you will be humble and quiet if you are meek and reverence creatures; you will be ready to bear others' burdens if you are of those who mourn because of their love and sympathy; you will remove strife if you hunger and thirst after God's justice, and still more if you are filled with divine mercy and pity; you will have power over others if you are clean

of heart and mind. And then, finally, wisdom will tell you
"how or what you shall answer and what you shall say";
wisdom will tell you, now eager to love and help and serve,
how to do it.

Let us think a little of what it means to be a peace-maker
in the life of the family. It is wisdom that most fully and
perfectly makes peace there; because wisdom removes the
ultimate ground and occasion of those clashes of mind and
will that arise too often from an inability to see the manifold
in terms of the One, to see all secondary issues in terms of
the final purpose of the home, the love and the glory of
God. But again, it is the quality of the child-life that makes
peace in the home; discord comes of stubborn self-assertion,
and though you can say that this self-assertion is the defect
of a quality—for you help to create the life of the family
best if you can contribute something of your own, if you
have initiative and a mind of your own—still it must remain
a defect unless there goes with this power to create the sense
of the unity of the family and of the final purpose of the
family—only, that is, if initiative is combined with docility
to the laws which govern initiative.

You create peace in the home by being yourself at peace,
though, of course, it is equally true that you learn to be at
peace yourself by striving to bring peace to the home; you
create joy by being yourself filled with joy. Again and
again we come back to the same principle: it is what you
are that matters most. The vocation of every christian as
such is to bring joy into the lives of those with whom he
comes in contact, and, above all, into the life of his own
home. But you cannot do this self-consciously; there is
nothing more depressing than the empty, self-conscious
bonhomie which is paraded as a studied programme, and in
no way reflects the state of mind and heart behind it. But
even where there is real affection, goodwill is not enough:
you need wisdom. There is such a thing as misplaced
jocularity; there are times when it can be a social crime to
be bonhomous at the breakfast-table. You need under-

standing, you need a sense of what is right at a given moment, or your goodwill may lead to disaster. Some people have this social sense, and know by instinct what to do; others are less favoured and must labour to acquire it; but all need the gift of wisdom, in any case, to unify their social life, to make all that they do a means not only to the immediate peace and well-being of the family but to its final happiness in heaven.

For it is possible to confuse the establishment of real peace with a cowardly avoidance of all issues, just as it is possible to confuse love with unprincipled kindliness. You must labour and pray for that peace which the world cannot give; and you will find it, not in compromise, not in always giving way to the immediate desires of the moment for the sake of a quiet life, but only by establishing the condition of peace, which is charity. And charity is not a vague term; it does not mean an easy-going amiability; on the contrary. It is a question of the will : thou shalt love the Lord thy God; thou shalt love thy neighbour; and in each case to love is to will the good of the other. That is why love is sometimes super-ficially and apparently hard : you want the good of the other so much that you are prepared to see him suffer if necessary, however much it hurts him, and you.

And so with peace; St. Thomas is quite clear : if you want peace within yourself you must unify all desires, which means that you must make all desires the aspects of one single desire, which means, in its turn, that you must love —you must will to obey—God, above all things. And if you want peace with and in your family, it is the same thing : you must want their good as much as you want your own; you must drive out selfishness and envy and jealousy and spite, and learn the meaning of the love that serves; and this you will do if you have the first kind of peace, because then will see the good of the family as part of that will of God which it is your supreme desire to fulfil.

But to do that is to live in the present : you know and recognize the presence of God in the midst of your family, and His continuous providence for it; you are at peace within yourself in the fullest sense because you are content to do the work of the present moment and let God provide for the future. " Be not solicitous "; it does not mean, of course, that you must take no thought at all for the morrow; to do that is part of the vocation of family life. But it does mean that when you have taken all prudent measures, when you have done what you can with the means that God has given you, then you refuse to worry, to be agitated, to make yourself miserable with imagined future woes or present difficulties. God has care of us : that is the visible demonstration of charity that you find in those christian homes where the lovers and makers of peace abide, the people in whom the gifts of the Spirit shine in splendour. God has care of us : and therefore even though times are incredibly hard, and they have to work all day and most of the night to make ends meet, and there seems never any security for the morrow, still they are filled with joy.* And with that peace which the world cannot give.

Wisdom means the ability to take the long view about everything; and that is, again, why wisdom and peace go together. If you are hopelessly upset by every transient ill-fortune; if you are thrown off your balance by every threat of trouble in the future, however remote; if you are endlessly worried about the state of your own soul and the perils which may beset it, instead of trying to love God and living in the trust which is begotten of love; then of course you are not at peace. But wisdom teaches you to look beyond these fears and timidities to the great lines of the eternal design, and the great power and love and protection

* Most of us, it is true, find that not only great sorrow but ill-health, drudgery, fatigue as well can make any feeling of joy impossible for us. Yet even we can discover the difference between the blank despair which these things are capable of bringing upon us and the peace with which a sense of God's presence can alleviate them ; and if we knew this presence as vividly as the saints we should know their unquenchable joy as well. " He who can bear suffering well," says Suso, " receives in this world a portion of the reward of his sufferings, for he finds peace and joy in all things."

of the everlasting arms; and then you have within you a peace which nothing can dismay, because you know that nothing can separate you from the charity of God which is in Christ Jesus our Lord.

So it will be given you in that hour what you shall say: and not only in the times of crisis, when you are faced with some equivalent of synagogues and magistrates. It will be given you, if you have ears to hear, what you shall say and what you shall do always, at every hour and in all circumstances: you will have a social sense greater than that which some have by nature and others by hard-won experience; you will have a *divine* sense of what love demands, and you will bring joy into the lives of your brethren because you yourself will be filled with the glowing light of the Godhead.

The gift of wisdom, then, enables us to act not only in the power but in the wisdom of Christ. And it is this wisdom, this sense of the nearness of the guiding hand of God, which explains the much misunderstood doctrine of " indifference " and " abandonment to the will of God." If you take these without the burning love and the divine wisdom which make them positive and creative things, you distort and indeed destroy them. " Teach us to care and not to care." First you must have the love which embraces all things, but which sees things aright, in God: you must live, and love, in the present. We live in the world of time, the world in which things are ceaselessly fading and passing away, and the insecurity of the presence of what we love lies heavy upon us. But that is only one side of the picture. Things which in themselves are fleeting exist also in the mind of God, and in the mind of God they eternally abide. For the life of God is the eternal " now ": the single infinite moment in which there is neither past nor future but all things are equally and for ever present. We, for our part, must see the tapestry of time piecemeal, as though we walked along beside it and could see only the part immediately before our eyes; but the eyes of God see the thing simultaneously in its wholeness, so that events which to us are remote in the past or unpredictably in the future are to Him no more remote or unreal than the actual moment of this our temporal present. In the mind of God, then, we must not suppose that things come to be or pass away; we must not suppose that there the flower fades and ceases to exist, the dead animal is as lost as it is to the world of time. For us there is inescapably the torment of the finite mind; but we are given this gift of wisdom to help us to see *quasi oculo Dei,* to have, in our own finite way, a dim perception of the way of the mind and the heart of God; and when we apply this to the world about us it can give us courage and comfort for the tyranny of time. We cannot have God's vision of things; but we can know about it, and realize that it means that there is a sense in which, when the flower fades and dies, it none the less has not wholly sunk into nothingness. And so, when the things you love are taken from you, you need not be sunk in utter misery and despair; because in spite of your sorrow you know that they are not wholly lost, you know that in eternity nothing is lost; you know that, could you share the life of the eternal present, you would find them there in the infinite reality of the heart of God. And in so far as you learn to listen to, and to live by, the wisdom of the Spirit, you learn to think thus of things precisely because you learn to see them and love them not apart from God but in God and for God : you learn to leave them to God, and to leave your love of them to God : it is all in His hands, they are in His hands, you yourself are in His hands; and so the transitoriness of earthly life begins to be in a sense a matter of indifference to you, not because you come to the soured conclusion that since nothing can last nothing can matter, but, on the contrary, because you realize that things have all the importance of the eternal present, and that that importance confers on them a kind of abidingness which heals and consoles your spirit, and you have with your sorrow a peace and a joy which cannot be taken from you, where otherwise, perhaps, you would only have despair.

It is the same with what is called, rather unfortunately in English, abandonment to divine Providence. It is an unfortunate word, because to us it suggests a purely negative and sombre state of affairs. It is exactly the opposite. It includes, first of all, the idea of a total loving acceptance of the will of God; this we thought of at the beginning of the book : the total destruction of self-will, the stripping of the self of all its independence and pride, and, on the other hand, the whole-hearted acceptance of all that God wills for us because it *is* His will—an acceptance that is not just a passive resignation in the ordinary colloquial sense of the word, but rather an active holding out of one's hands to it, a positive willing, and therefore an attitude of loving gratitude to God for all that He sends whether it be joy or pain. And therefore, for that very reason, this abandonment includes the idea which is implied in the word "abandon": something entirely care-free, spontaneous, without reserve in the sense, let us say, in which conventional reserve can shackle inspiration or gaiety. When you have the sense of God's providence guiding every event, however insignificant, the conviction (begotten of wisdom) that all things work together unto good, and the humble childlike trust that if you love as much as you can and do the best you can, God will guide you in all your words and works, then, of course, you are abandoned to His will in the sense that you become free of fret or worry, you cast your care on God, you do not scheme to circumvent His designs for, on the contrary, you love and welcome all that He gives you precisely as His gift whether pleasant or painful, you are poor and meek and hunger after justice and are clean of heart and your will is to do God's will because, through your love, in all things and events you see God. And therefore you have this element of "abandon" in the other sense : you are filled with joy and happiness because you are entirely carefree—*la sua voluntade è nostra pace.*

To have this fullness of peace and wisdom is, of course, to serve more than the immediate family. By being thus you will act always, because of what you are, in the wisdom as well as the power of Christ: you will act for the *totus Christus,* and for the whole family of mankind. All that we were thinking before of mercy and pity finds its fruition here: " to make peace, either in oneself or among others," says St. Thomas, " shows one to be a follower of God, who is the God of unity and peace." You comfort—you console and strengthen—by making the world about you a world of peace; and this you can only do by learning gradually and with ceaseless travail to live wholly for God and in His love, so as to become, in the end, transparent of God, showing forth in yourself the peace of God, and thus bringing your brethren, perhaps in great multitudes down the ages, to the feet of Christ. But only so can you do it: only by being a man of peace; and the way to that is prayer and humility, vision and love.

It is a lovely epitaph to be called a peace-maker. Other greatness can win the honour of men; this greatness wins their love. And why? Perhaps because this greatness is essentially the fruit of pity—for it is when you are very wise and very humble that you can pity, not before—and pity, the divine pity, is what compels love. To be a lover and maker of peace is the vocation of every christian as such: but each beatitude depends on those which have gone before: you must be poor and meek and clean of heart and merciful, and then you will have within you the Will which is our peace. " The highest place in the royal palace," says St. Thomas, referring to the second half of this beatitude, " belongs to the king's son ": but let us remember that it was when he had thrown away everything and had wed the lady Poverty and fallen in love with all humanity and all reality in the immensity of God, and gone forth naked—

abandoned, care-free—to serve them, that Francis sang his song of pride and joy and glory : I am a king's son.

A.   WISDOM AND THE PRAYER OF UNION

For wisdom is more active than all active things : and reacheth everywhere by reason of her purity. For she is a vapour of the power of God and a certain pure emanation of the glory of the almighty God. . . . And being but one she can do all things : and remaining in herself the same she reneweth all things. . . . She is more beautiful than the sun, and above all the order of the stars : being compared with the light, she is found before it. For after this cometh night, but no evil can overcome wisdom.

WISDOM VII. 24 sqq.

Wisdom is the deepest and the loveliest of the gifts. It marks, in a sense, the end of that process we have been considering, the process which begins with the new birth in baptism : the death of the false self, the coming to be of the new self *in* God. It marks, therefore, the summit of both the child-life and of the life of maturity : the child-life, because there is the complete fulfilment of this gift when the soul is completely rapt in God, completely restored to oneness; the mature life, because this is the gift which enables us to judge all things by their " highest causes "— it is the gift which, when it is completely active in a man, makes him a *sage*. *Sapientis est ordinare* : it belongs to the wise man to put things in order; it belongs to the man who is wise with the wisdom of the Spirit, the wisdom which is " from above," to put things in their divine order, bringing the entire manifold of creation into unity so that " all things work together for good," but doing so not with the violence of regimentation but with divine reverence and pity for the lease of created things; for we are told of the divine wisdom that she " reacheth from end to end mightily," but also that " she ordereth all things sweetly."

Wisdom is the end of the process because in wisdom all the beatitudes are included, and all those good things are present which, without wisdom, are misinterpreted so that men follow after strange gods. The beatitudes have shown us those misinterpretations; but, as we have seen, the right use of instincts is not to destroy them but to heal and fulfil them. There is true wealth as well as illusory: " and if riches be desired in life, what is richer than wisdom, which maketh all things?" There is true power as well as false: and " if, then, your delight be in thrones and sceptres, O ye kings of the people, love wisdom, that you may reign for ever," for she is a " vapour of the power of God," she " can do all things," and no evil can overcome her. There is true glory as well as the glory that is vain; and we read " for her sake I shall have glory among the multitude, and honour with the ancients, though I be young." There is true plea- sure, and joy, and comfort; and we are told " when I go into my house I shall repose myself with her: for her con- versation hath no bitterness, nor her company any tedious- ness, but joy and gladness "; and she " will be a comfort in my cares and grief "; she is " more beautiful than the sun, and above all the order of the stars." There is that life of action which is not a distraction from the end, but an ex- pression of it: " and if a man loves justice, her labours have great virtues "; and " if sense do work, who is a more artful worker than she of those things that are?" There is the desire for knowledge and understanding and vision; and " all such things as are hidden and not foreseen I have learnt: for wisdom, which is the worker of all things, taught me." And lastly there is the hunger for that true peace which the world cannot give; and we read that by wisdom " I shall set the people in order, and nations shall be subject to me "; and that, where the inner peace of the spirit is concerned, " by wisdom they were healed, whoso- ever hath pleased Thee O Lord, from the beginning," and it is in wisdom that " thou shalt find rest in the latter end."

But how are all these things made one, and how are they to be acquired? " This also was a point of wisdom, to know whose gift it was. I went to the Lord, and besought Him,

and said with my whole heart: God of my fathers and Lord
of mercy . . . give me wisdom that sitteth by thy throne . . .
For I am thy servant and the son of thy handmaid, a weak
man and of short time, and falling short of the understanding of judgement and laws. For if one be perfect among the
children of men, yet if thy wisdom be not with him he shall
be nothing regarded." This is the wisdom which is " from
above."

Wisdom in general, as we have seen, is not in a vast store
of information, nor in scientific knowledge; it is not the
same thing as critical ability; it is not to be acquired simply
by character-training. It is the knowledge of things by their
highest and ultimate causes. But again there are degrees of
wisdom. You can have that wisdom which is natural knowledge of natural things: we call it philosophy, and it is very
great; but there is greater wisdom than that. You can have
that sort of wisdom which is discursive knowledge of supernatural things: we call it theology, and it is greater but not
the greatest. For you can have also that divine wisdom
which is supernatural experience of supernatural reality:
and this is the utmost height of the human spirit on earth
because it is not just reason-knowledge but love-knowledge,
a direct if obscure union with the Infinite, the knowledge
of the highest things in the sense that the knower is one in
the depths of his being with the Known. *Patiens divina*:
he knows because he *experiences* divine things.

That is why from this wisdom there is peace; because in
it all desires are made aspects of one desire; there is joy,
because in it there is a sense of the solution of even the
hardest and deepest problems of evil and pain; there is
abundance of life, because this wisdom is itself oneness with
the Infinite life; there is abundance of power, because to
experience divine things is to have the cosmic energy of
redemption within the self.

" I went to the Lord and besought him." The wisdom
which is from above is spoken of in the feminine; the word
itself is feminine. For this is not the masculine science, and

power of governance, which are conquered, acquired; it is
the wisdom that is received from above, given in love, not
taken possession of by the soul so much as brought forth
in the soul that is possessed by divinity. The soul is female
to God. The Son is the Wisdom of the Father : the Man,
but also the Eternal Child. But among creatures it is Mary
who is the supreme expression of the divine wisdom and its
supreme symbol, for in woman you have the identification
of child-life and maturity. Mary the Mother, Mary the
Bride : the first is the epitome of all human experience, the
mother of sorrows, the queen of the seven swords; the epitome of all that ordering of things, but ordering sweetly,
which is motherhood; the epitome of all the care and responsibility and pity of the bearer for the born. But the
second title is the key to the depth and the stillness and
the wonder : is what turns experience into gentleness, understanding into pity, governance into sweetness, responsibility into compassion, sorrow into joy. In the eyes of
the mother is the understanding of " the beginning, and
ending, and midst of the times "; but they are also and for
ever the eyes of the girl, the bride, who says " He that is
mighty hath done great things in me." To be like Mary
you must have wisdom and be able to say " I understand ";
but to be able to say that you must first say with her " Teach
me."

The soul is female to God. You must use to the full the
mental power that God has given you; you must acquire
wisdom and acquire it not least by the hard road of human
experience; but you need, more than all this, the wisdom
that is from above, and that wisdom can only be given you.
It is the divine wisdom that can " dispose all things
sweetly," that knows pity as well as order : the man who is
unsure of himself and his knowledge or competence blusters
and bullies; the wise man is gentle with other minds because he understands them, and patient with their defects
because he is sure of his own ground; he has the patience
of divine tolerance—which is so different from the unprin-

cipled tolerance which makes no distinction between truth
and falsehood—because he takes always the long view,
knows that good can come eventually from evil and truth
from falsehood, and can pity and help instead of condemning because he understands with what obstacles the human
mind and heart have to contend. His is not the remote
unreality of the academic philosopher nor the immersion in
the world of time of the superficial pleasure-seeker: he is
wholly in the eternal present because he lives in wisdom who
" remaineth in herself the same," but he is wholly in the
world of time also, because his wisdom is the wisdom that
serves the world. To dispose all things *sweetly*: that is the
test of the divine wisdom in practice. " Charity is kind,"
says St. Paul; and Ruysbroeck tells us simply : " Be kind,
be kind, and you will be saints." That is the quality in
the wisdom of the saints that gives them power—the power
to compel others to love what they love.

Wisdom is the fruit of love : we judge things as though
with the eyes of God because we are *one* with God. " An
emanation of the glory "; the men of prayer have spoken of
the spirit of man as a *scintilla Dei*, a spark thrown off, as it
were, from the infinite globe of fire, created into separateness—the spark is not the fire, the finite is not the Infinite—
and yet destined while still retaining its self-identity, to
return into the greater life of the One and the All, for only
there can it find its own fullness, its complete enhancement
and glory, of being.

Is this return a thing which only heaven can fulfil? Perfectly, yes : it can be fulfilled completely only in the glory
of the light inaccessible, when the eyes of the spirit behold
face to face the Unimaginable and are rapt in timeless ecstasy. But there are some who have known heaven on
earth : a beginning of beatitude is possible even this side
the grave. The divine life into which the sons of God are
re-born confers on them a new power : the power to apprehend the Godhead itself, present within them, as immediate object of knowledge and love. God is present within

them, not only as Creator of all that the soul is, but as that with which the spirit can be truly united, as that which the spirit can truly and immediately *experience*. "He that cleaveth to the Lord is *one spirit*." Those who have experienced these divine things tell us, in so far as human language can, how real and close a union this is. It is not yet to be described in terms of vision : that cannot be while they are still living the life of faith; but they convey to us something of its immediacy and intimacy by speaking of it in terms of the sense of touch. There is something much more here than the silence of deep understanding : it is the silence of the love that is too deep for words :

> Lost to all things and myself,
> And amid the lilies forgotten.

You are here in a realm beyond ideas : "What agony," says St. Teresa "for the soul to return to reason." You are in the realm of the highest form of love-knowledge, apart from the vision of God. Think for a moment of human ecstasy : the word conveys the idea of being "outside the self," because the intensity of love and joy is such as to fill the self completely and exclusively with the realization of the other, and of the greater life into which one is thus caught up and transformed; there is a real, if momentary, self oblivion, a forgetfulness too of everything except this immediate and wholly absorbing reality, and perhaps for this moment the whole personality is really made one and made whole and made wholly expressive in a wordless affirmation of surrender to this greater reality into which it is absorbed. In some such terms the mystics have described the reality of the prayer of union : the absorption, the oblivion of everything except the supreme Reality, the sense of oneness, the sense of utter fullness of spirit—"I have found Him whom my soul loveth : I have held Him and I will not let Him go."

Sometimes the intensity of this experience produces those

physical effects which are too often supposed to be the essentials of the highest states of prayer: they are entirely irrelevant and accidental; they merely mean that the body is not strong enough to bear the experience given, the life imparted: they are on the same level as the momentary loss of consciousness which can be produced by any intense joy or sorrow. The essence of the prayer of union is precisely the *union* of spirit with Spirit. But we have to remember, also, that this supreme experience must, of its nature, be transitory: there are limits to the joy as well as the suffering that human beings can bear. It can be no more than a moment in life: but of course it must necessarily colour and transform the rest of life. For the moment, you leave the prayer of petition and sorrow and the rest; but only for the moment. Wisdom is "more active than all active things": if you are given this supreme prayer it is as a sharing in Christ's eternal adoration of the Father, and therefore as a sharing also in His redemption of the world.

We come back to the christian ideal of action as the overflow and expression of contemplation: if you are caught up in the power of the Spirit even to the seventh heaven it is that you may then share more fully, with greater power, in the redemptive activity of Christ in the world. Father Vincent McNabb, preaching to some of his fellow Dominicans, once said: "The world is waiting for those who love it; if you don't love the world, don't preach to it: preach to yourself." The primary thing, if you are to be a preacher, is to have the truth; and since we all in some way preach, though not perhaps in words, it is the truth that we primarily need. But for your preaching to have a deep and lasting effect you need more than an intellectual apprehension of the truth; you need the wisdom which is from above, the wisdom that makes you yourself one with the truth in heart as well as in mind. Then you have the power that can hope to drive out prejudice and make way for the truth: you have that inner power which is love, which draws all things to Christ.

"She is more beautiful than the sun, and . . . being compared with the light, she is found before it. For after this cometh night; but no evil can overcome wisdom." When you have the wisdom of the Spirit you have the source itself of all serenity; you have also the fine flower of fortitude. Nothing can overcome it : you are not worried as to what you shall say, for it is given you what you shall say; you are not dismayed by obstacles, for you know that you live in the life and power of Him who has overcome the world, Him with whom all things are possible. So you yourself are still with the stillness of deep night, yet more active than all active things because of the fire that blazes in you, and from you to the world. "Being but one, she can do all things, and remaining in herself the same, she reneweth all things." So we pray in the prayer to the holy Spirit : Send forth thy Spirit and they shall be re-created, and Thou shalt renew the face of the earth. And so, when we have asked for the gift of true wisdom, we go on to ask for what necessarily goes with it; that we may always "rejoice in His holy consolations"—His strengthening solace and renewal—through Christ our Lord. Amen.

B. THE SACRAMENT OF THE PRIESTHOOD

For winter is now past, the rain is over and gone. The flowers have appeared in our land : the time of pruning is come : the voice of the turtle is heard in our land.

CANT. II. 11-12.

It is the old traditional catholic doctrine that all the faithful share in the priesthood of Christ. Let us think briefly, first of all, of what the official priesthood means; we shall then be able to apply something of what we have discovered to the common priesthood of the laity in which we all must share.

The essence of the priesthood is the power to say Mass: to be the mouthpiece of the words of consecration which change the bread and wine into the Body and Blood of Christ, and then to administer to the faithful the sacrament of the sacrificed Christ. And why? Because essentially the Church is the torrent of divine life and power which flows ceaselessly into the world, to heal and restore it: as all the other functions of the priesthood, the teaching office, the pastoral charge, the administration of the other sacraments, are all grouped about and centre in this supreme office of offering Mass, so all the things which make up the Church's life, doctrinal, pastoral, disciplinary, are aspects of this essential fact, that the Church is the continuation of the Christ-life on earth, teaching, healing, empowering; it is the storehouse of the energy and power of good which must combat the power of evil to the end, and which, as it triumphs over the dark power, makes all things new.

But that means that the apostolate is of the essence of the Church's life, because it is bound up with the Eucharist. The duty of the priest is first to say *Hoc est corpus meum,* This is My Body, turning to God with the people; but then he must say also *Hoc est corpus eius,* This is His Body, turning to the people with God. And as we have seen, it is the whole of creation that must be brought to the Mass to be healed and sanctified: beyond the immediate assistants there is the whole body of the faithful; beyond the faithful there is the whole of creation, still in travail even till now. So, to express the priesthood and the Church in general you have to think of a double duty: to bring God to the world, to bring the world to God.

In that double movement the laity share. The old doctrine of the common priesthood has found in these latter days a new expression in terms of catholic action. The priest is in an official sense a mediator, turning to God with the people, turning to the people with God; but the whole company of the faithful must also mediate in a different way, turning first to God as a family, a unity, and then, still a family,

turning in the life and power of God to the greater family
of mankind and all creation, witnessing, blessing, showing
forth the abundance of life and power and love and through
them drawing all things to Christ. But again this mediatorship is centred in the Mass: it is a sacrificial life that is to
be shown, unself-consciously but powerfully, to the world.
That is the essence of the common priesthood. "We are all
anointed into one holy priesthood," says St. Ambrose,
"whenever we offer ourselves as sacrifices to God." And
St. Leo asks: "What is there so priestly . . . as to bring to
God from the altar of the heart the immaculate sacrifice of
christian piety?" The common priesthood is the priesthood
of service: a service sanctified by the spirit of worship and
of sacrifice.

Once again we return to the christian view of the life of
action as the overflow and expression of contemplation. If
the phrase "catholic action," is interpreted as meaning that
the way to serve the Church is to be endlessly active and to
let contemplation take care of itself, then the glory of the
common priesthood must necessarily be lost. There must
always be enough inner life to vivify the external life of
action, otherwise it will be weak and superficial and perhaps harmful, however much goodwill may be put into it.
You share in the priesthood of Christ first of all if you share
in the prayer of Christ. There are some in the Church
whose whole function is to be, in a phrase of Père Ser-
tillanges, "beings of praise": the contemplative religious
whose primary work is the *opus Dei,* the liturgy. They are
in a special sense the Church's worship, and therefore the
Church's powerhouse; but their life is something in which
we all have to share. Whenever you assist at Mass or at
the Divine Office, whenever you pray, as you always in fact,
as a christian do, within the framework of the total prayer
of the Church, you join in that official act of worship, and
you share in the primary function of being the storehouse
of the divine power. But to do that is itself an apostolate,
and the necessary condition of all other apostolic activities.

Worship is an apostolate because it is a worship of love: we cannot pray as christians at all unless in our prayer the travail of all creation is at least implicitly expressed.

But then, when this primary condition of prayer is at least beginning to be fulfilled, then it is possible to turn to the priesthood of service: bringing God to the world, not in the official and literal manner of the priest with the Eucharist, but in the sense that the service of love spreads light and joy in the world and the light is the Life.

To feed the hungry and give drink to the thirsty, to clothe the naked and harbour the harbourless: all these works of mercy are ways of sharing in the common priesthood; and so are all the ways in which the faithful take their immensely important share in the work of making known the truth of the Gospel and making known the love that the Gospel reveals. The tasks of the common priesthood change with the changing circumstances of life: perhaps the type of all such tasks today is the sacrificial work which attempts to redeem industrialism from within, in the power of Christ the Worker. But all work can be in some degree a fulfilment of this priesthood, provided always that it is turned into worship and so becomes the expression of love. And again the two things, work and worship, are mutually inter-active: you make your worship complete when you make it a part of your work for the world; you make your work complete when you turn it into loving service of the world and so into worship of the Redeemer of the world. You can praise Him with harp and timbrel; but you can praise Him, too, as Mary His mother did, with all the common daily work of your hands; you can praise Him with all the cares and drudgery, you can praise him with all the fun and laughter, that come your way, if you take these things as a love-gift from Him and make them a love-gift to your family.

But the christian's family, once again, is the world. There can be no limit to the scope of apostolic activity, because of the divine *immensitas* of charity. There is a difference here between those who are called to the sacrament of marriage and those who are called to the religious life of the cloister. These latter must, *ex officio,* substitute for a life of love rounded immediately by their own particular home (even though, as we have seen, the home has its vocation in the world beyond) a life of love which immediately embraces all humanity. No need to stress their tremendous need of abundance of life and power. Perhaps it is easy to love all humanity in the abstract—and from the point of view of humanity it is likely to be valueless; but to love all humanity in the concrete, to love all men and women, is beyond the power of man. How, then, are they to hope for the life and the power? Because of the special relationship in which, if they are faithful to their calling, they stand to God.

In the normal way, men and women are completed in marriage : but notice that this substantial completion is of its nature limited—you are completed in this particular framework of love and shared life, and it is your boundary, even though it then looks beyond itself. The religious life has no such limitation, glorious though that limitation is : the monk and the nun miss the normal way of completion, and if they misunderstand their vocation they become in consequence shrunken and desiccated; but if they understand it aright and are faithful to the last ounce of their energy they find not a loss but an immeasurable gain. St. Thomas is accustomed to speak of God as possessing the qualities or powers of creatures *virtualiter eminenter* : not having the thing itself as it is in us, since that would be a limitation, but having it virtually, having the power of producing the same effect, and having it in a pre-eminent way, since what, for example, is for us a matter of energy and labour is for Him simply the effortless *fiat* of infinite will. So it is with those who are called to forgo the completion of married life : their denial is but an aspect of a far greater affirmation; for the fullness of life which married love brings to these others is meant to be found for them in the greater fullness of their life with God. And it is a fullness which of its nature is such as to be expressed, not in the small world of the home, but in the universality of creation. They, too, are meant to share a life of love, and be completed by it; but it is a love whose purpose and fulfilment alike are not *these* children begotten of *this* father, but *all* created things, the children of the heavenly Father. So they can give all to the world because they have been given all by God; their vocation is to be identified with Mary in her universal pity because they are to be identified with her in her divine wisdom; and they are to share this divine wisdom because they are to share with her the prayer of union: they are to share with her, though in so different a way, that immediacy of relationship between themselves and the Spirit which implies a complete possession by the Spirit—a possession which completes them precisely as accepting, and feeling responsibility for, all created thing as their own.

All that is the special glory, and the terrifying responsibility, of the priest and the religious. But we all must share in it, because we all must share in the common priesthood of the faithful. Married love has its own immediate and essential purpose; but, as we have seen, it looks beyond itself to the world without, and it looks to the world without because it first looks up to God. We are called to the substance of the prayer of union and the life of union; and human love is only fulfilled when it is part of that mightier love, when the single living spark that is two-in-unity returns to the infinite Fire. And then, so enhanced and empowered and intensified, it returns to the world of men, to share in its own particular way in the universal love and universal pity—a love and a pity which, it is true, are to be shown for the most part implicitly, or at least within the relatively small circle of immediate neighbours and friends, but which, none the less, cannot be circumscribed, cannot be limited to any circle, any nation, any race, in the inner readiness of the heart to love and serve. That is why in married life there must be the spirit of the three monastic vows: there must be poverty of spirit, there must be the chastity of the temperate and the clean of heart, there must be the obedience of those who love all the things that God loves, and whose joy is to fulfil His will in serving them.

The soul is female to God. Our Lady is the universal Mother in this sense also that we have, all of us, to learn from her as from a model of what we are to be. The whole train of thought we have been following through these pages is fulfilled pre-eminently in her. Think of the glorious song of praise that she sang when Elizabeth saluted the majesty of her motherhood : it is a triumphant assertion of the re-birth of mankind into the new and infinite life : the winter is past, the rain is over and gone, because man is no longer doomed to the misery of loneliness, the Centre of life is restored to him, he can be fulfilled to infinity because he can lose his life, to find it again in God. If you read through the verses of the *Magnificat* you find in them almost a summary of the beatitudes; you find certainly that ringing note of love and wonder and humility and happiness about which they tell us.

" My soul doth magnify the Lord, and my spirit hath rejoiced in God my Saviour " : at the very beginning there is the primary lesson of poverty of spirit, the fixing of the eyes not on the self but on God. " Because he hath regarded the humility of his handmaid " (the meekness of the truly happy) " for behold from henceforth all generations shall call me blessed." How she must have trembled as she spoke the lovely boast, trembled with love and wonder, but most of all with the bewilderment of humility : for it is " because he that is mighty hath done great things in me; and holy is his name. And his mercy."—his comfort—" is from generation to generation, to them that fear him "—and fearing, are able to mourn. " He hath shewed might in his arm : he hath scattered the proud in the conceit of their heart. He hath put down the mighty "—those who seek not the inner power of love but the external might that feeds pride and is fed by injustice—" from their seat and hath exalted the humble," the little ones, the clean of heart who have the docility of the child. " He hath filled the hungry with good things "—those who are hungry because of their suffering of injustice, those who mourn, those who themselves hunger and thirst after justice;—" and the rich," those who treat created things as means to their own pleasure or profit—" he hath sent empty away. He hath received Israel His servant, being mindful of His mercy " because to be a servant, to be a humble instrument of His mercy, and so to bring to the world His life and His light and His peace, is in itself to receive His mercy in all its fullness. You must struggle and fight and persevere with all your strength; but when you think that any success, any goodness, is achieved you must say " *He* that is mighty hath done great things *in me, and holy is his* name."

" For I am thy servant and the son of thy handmaid, a weak man, and of short time, and falling short of the understanding of judgement and laws." Mary is the universal Mother, and therefore we who are her children are to try to model ourselves upon her; " for it is she," as is said of the wisdom with which the Church identifies her, " that teacheth the knowledge of God "; it is she who in her gesture of humble and proud acceptance at the Annunciation symbolizes for us the response of the creature to the healing and ennobling touch of God. From her we learn to be happy, for in her is the selfless poverty of spirit that makes her a Mother, the childlike meekness that makes her the Virgin-bride of the Infinite, the sacrificial mourning that gives her the strength of the Tower of Ivory and makes her the Cause of our Joy, the hunger and thirst for God's will that makes her Mirror of Justice, the pity that makes her the Comfort of the Afflicted, the cleanness of heart that makes her the Seat of Wisdom, the flawless inner peace that entitles her to be called the Queen of Peace.

And to those who know that to love and revere her is only to do the greater honour to her Son she is also to be greeted with one of the loveliest of her titles, the Morning Star, the star that heralds the dawn of the Word in the world; for it

is through the birth of her Son that the whole world is re-
born and renewed; it is through the glory of her selfless
magnificat that the Light comes into the world and makes
all things new. In her, therefore, is all the joy of the life of
worship, joy because what was lost is recovered, what was
dead is quickened to new life; joy because even in spite of
sin and suffering the world is lovely again, for His feet have
trodden it; joy because winter is now past, the rain is over
and gone, the flowers have appeared in our land—and in
the priestly bestowal of life which brings about the re-
flowering of the earth she, and all her children who follow
her, share and are glorified; joy finally because this is not
an end but a beginning, the joyful sacrifice that precedes the
eternal banquet and must be offered till the end when the
day break and the shadows retire; for beyond there lies the
fullness of glory, the blazing splendour of the Sun of the
eternal noon, the new heaven and new earth that are the
tabernacle of God with men, and He shall wipe away all
tears from their eyes and there shall be neither mourning
nor crying nor any other sorrow, for the former things shall
have passed away, and they shall see His face, and night
shall be no more.

MERE CHRISTIANITY
C. S. Lewis

MERE CHRISTIANITY is a revised and amplified edition, with a new Introduction of C. S. Lewis's three famous books, *Broadcast Talks*, *Christian Behaviour* and *Beyond Personality*. Thus are gathered together for the first time at a popular price Dr. Lewis's modern revaluations of Christian apologetics, ethics and theology.

THE SCREWTAPE LETTERS
C. S. Lewis

On its first appearance THE SCREWTAPE LETTERS was immediately recognised as a milestone in the history of popular theology. Its new appearance in paper covers and at a price accessible to all serves to bring it to the notice of a whole new reading public, whose first encounter with that elderly devil, Screwtape, with his witty and profound analysis of Christian strength and weaknesses outlined in letters to his young nephew, will surely help them on their way as others have already been so signally helped.

LETTERS TO YOUNG CHURCHES
J. B. Phillips

" The Epistles of the New Testament are here translated into vigorous, contemporary English, and yet the fidelity of this version to the original is remarkable. This book makes a first-rate introduction to the faith."   *The Church Times*

MAKING MEN WHOLE
J. B. Phillips

IN MAKING MEN WHOLE, J. B. Phillips has given us one of his finest books—a vigorous and searching appraisal of the place of both Christian and non-Christian in the modern world and of their part of God's purpose.